The Fratelli Camisa
Cookery Book

Elizabeth Camisa was born in Staffordshire and moved in 1979 to London, where she now lives with her husband Francesco and their baby daughter Sofia. The Camisa family own two specialist food shops in the West End of London, the first of which was established in 1929, and she has been involved in all aspects of the family business, including catering, for a number of years. She has been inspired to write this book by her marriage into an Italian family, her love of cooking and her first-hand knowledge of Italy, its people and, of course, its food!

ELIZABETH CAMISA

THE FRATELLI CAMISA COOKERY BOOK

A COLLECTION OF AUTHENTIC FAMILY RECIPES

Illustrated by Phillida Gili

PENGUIN BOOKS

PENGUIN BOOKS

Published by the Penguin Group
27 Wrights Lane, London w8 5tz, England
Viking Penguin Inc., 40 West 23rd Street, New York, New York 10010, USA
Penguin Books Australia Ltd, Ringwood, Victoria, Australia
Penguin Books Canada Ltd, 2801 John Street, Markham, Ontario, Canada l3r 1b4
Penguin Books (NZ) Ltd, 182–190 Wairau Road, Auckland 10, New Zealand

Penguin Books Ltd, Registered Offices: Harmondsworth, Middlesex, England

First published 1989
1 3 5 7 9 10 8 6 4 2

Made and printed in Great Britain by
Richard Clay Ltd, Bungay, Suffolk

Filmset in Monophoto Bembo

For my father Janko Djuranovic
and my daughter Sofia, who was born
during the writing of the book

CONTENTS

ACKNOWLEDGEMENTS

I should like to express my special thanks to my husband Francesco for his help and support in the writing of this book.

I should also like to thank my in-laws Ennio, Ines and Alberto Camisa for teaching me so much about Italian food, to my own family for their encouragement, and to Zia Antonia, who has given me so much inspiration.

Thank you too to Phillida Gili for her enthusiasm in producing such wonderful illustrations, to Esther Sidwell at Penguin Books and to Carol Magee, who typed the manuscript.

INTRODUCTION

When the first Fratelli Camisa shop was established in Soho in 1929 it catered mainly for the local Italian community. Today there is enormous interest in foreign food in England and the business has expanded to cope with the increased demand. The shop is filled with products imported direct from Italy and customers can enjoy browsing around, smelling the cheeses and salami and the rich aroma of freshly ground Italian coffee, and investigating the dried *funghi*, the fresh pasta, the dark green olive oils and the wide variety of Italian wines. The invitation to cook is irresistible.

For many people, all too familiar with English-style spaghetti bol and American deep-filled pizza, a first visit to Italy is a revelation: colourful fruit and vegetable stalls piled high with juicy peaches and melons, purple aubergines and knobbly tomatoes streaked in green and orange; little grocers' shops with salami hanging from the ceiling and at the counter a variety of whole cheeses from the region which you will be invited to taste; bakers selling their own bread, as well as tempting pastries and vivid fruit tarts. All fresh local produce, cut to order.

The cookery of Italy is based on local seasonal produce, flavoured with fresh herbs and good-quality olive oil, and depends for its flavour on the quality of the raw ingredients. There is a great diversity of recipes, reflecting the different regional traditions and the variety of foods available in the different parts of the country: dairy foods from the Alps in the north, fish from the immensely long sea coast, fruit and vegetables ripened by the Mediterranean sun . . .

In Italy, a good cook is greatly appreciated by her family,

for Italians love to eat well, and good cooking is not reserved for special occasions. For most Italians lunch is the main meal of the day, and shops and offices are closed for several hours at midday so that – even today, when many women work outside the home – there is ample time for the meal to be cooked and enjoyed to the full.

Italian meals are relaxed and informal, and the food unpretentious. I have been delighted, when I have taken English friends to Italy, to see how quickly they have adapted to the Italian life-style, with the long leisurely lunch, huge dishes of pasta, steaks sizzling on a stone in the sunshine, crisp fresh salad and a tiny cup of black coffee, followed by a quick siesta in the shade.

On Sundays and holidays, families will join together and the meal becomes a social occasion. Even the preparations may turn into a social gathering as two or three cooks get together to produce an impromptu meal for friends and family. I have enjoyed many such meals, often eaten outside in the moonlight, with a few bottles of wine, music, singing and perhaps some *grappa*.

Food varies greatly from one region to another, which is hardly surprising, as until 1861 Italy was made up of independent states, each with its own culinary traditions. As you travel through Italy you will come across many different local specialities, as well as a wide variety of local wines. Even the traditional dishes which are known throughout the country vary from one region to another, as they are adapted to suit the ingredients that are available locally. In the north the food is richer, making more use of meat and dairy produce; in the south, meat is used more sparingly.

*

Over the years that I have been involved with Fratelli Camisa – buying, selling and catering – I have come to love Italian food; my intention in writing this book is to pass on some of the recipes that I have collected from my Italian relatives, particularly from my mother-in-law, whose advice and expertise have been invaluable. These are practical, unpretentious recipes for the kind of food that is cooked in Italian homes.

Many of the recipes are from the province of Parma, one of the towns on the ancient Via Emilia, for that is where most of my husband's family come from. (The region and its people are portrayed in Eric Newby's *Love and War in the Apennines*, in which he describes how he was sheltered by the Italian peasants when he was hiding from German soldiers during the war.) Parma is in Emilia-Romagna, which is renowned throughout Italy for its good food and good cooking. This is the region which produces Parmigiano-Reggiano cheese (parmesan), Parma ham and the sparkling Lambrusco wine. The soil is rich and fertile, and some of the finest mushrooms in Italy grow in the foothills of the Apennines. Butter and cheese are generously used, and there are many local varieties of sausages and cured meats. Fresh pasta is very popular as a first course, and there are many delectable sauces for pasta and a wide variety of stuffed pasta dishes, such as *tortelli di erbette*.

Because Italian cookery is generally uncomplicated, there are many recipes here that can be undertaken by beginner cooks with good results. And if you are a vegetarian, or want to cut down on the meat content of your meals, Italian cooking has much to offer. Indeed, it is now thought that the traditional diet of the Italian south, sparing of meat and dairy foods but high in fish, vegetables, cereals and olive oil, is one of the healthiest in Europe.

A word of warning. It is best not to try a particular recipe unless you have the correct ingredients – you may find the results disappointing if you use substitutes. Of course, you may want to adjust the amount of herbs or seasoning to suit your own tastes, but you must have the correct cut of veal if you are going to make Osso Bucco or Scaloppine alla Marsala. Often I decide what I am going to make *after* I have been shopping, so that I can take advantage of anything that looks particularly good – some fresh fish perhaps, or some specially inviting vegetable.

It is important, too, that you allow yourself plenty of time for your cooking. For one thing, you will get much more pleasure from it if you can relax and take your time – and the food will be better too. If a recipe stipulates long slow simmering so that the flavours of the different ingredients can blend together and develop, you obviously won't get as good a result if you skimp on the time.

I hope you will enjoy cooking and eating the recipes in this book. If you have good fresh ingredients, you do not need exceptional culinary skills to make a really delicious Italian meal.

Buon appetito!

EQUIPMENT

I have listed below those items of kitchen equipment that are particularly useful in Italian cooking. Few are absolutely essential, but having the right tool for the job can save much time and effort.

FOOD PROCESSORS

A food processor would definitely be one of my first choices: it chops and shreds vegetables quickly and efficiently; it makes excellent dough for bread and pizza; and it chops and minces meat for sauces and stuffings. It can be used to make pasta dough, too, but this is better done by hand or with a pasta machine, either electric or manual.

If you do not possess a food processor and are thinking of buying one, do be sure first that you will use it fully and that you have room for it in your kitchen – there is nothing worse than having to wade through a cupboard, emptying out most of the contents, in order to get at the food processor. If you do decide to buy one, have a good look round first and select the one that is best fitted to your requirements, as there are many different models on the market, and they can be very expensive.

PASTA MACHINES

Pasta machines are now available in this country. Both the manual pasta machines and the small electric ones for domestic use are very efficient and fast, and take much of the hard work out of rolling out the pasta and cutting it to shape. The manual one is quite reasonably priced; the electric one is expensive, so before you rush out to buy one make sure that you are going to be a serious pasta maker!

Pasta machine

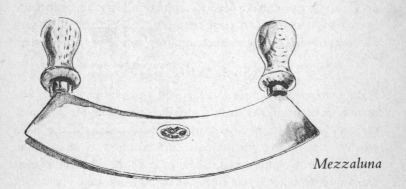

Mezzaluna

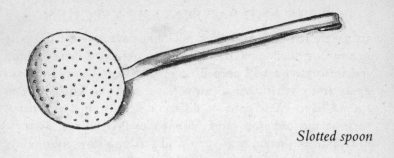

Slotted spoon

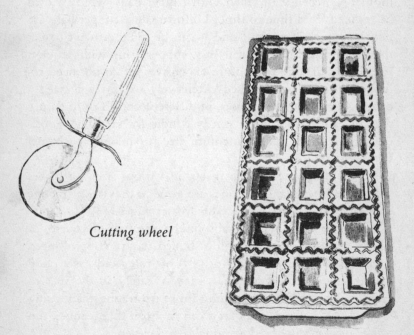

Cutting wheel

Ravioli tray

POTS AND PANS IN THE KITCHEN

Everyone has their favourite pots and pans, even if the only reason for their preference is the colour. When cooking Italian food you will need little in the way of pots and pans apart from what you already have in your kitchen. You should have a few pans of different sizes with heavy bases, such as the cast-iron ones with enamelled linings, as these distribute and retain heat very well for long slow simmering. My mother-in-law has often told me that the shelves of her mother's kitchen were filled with copper pans, which had to be re-lined from time to time. Unfortunately copper pans are now extremely expensive and it can be quite difficult to get them re-lined, but you can buy copper pans with stainless steel inners that are even more expensive but do not need re-lining. Frying-pans are used extensively so you will need a couple, also with heavy bases, in different sizes. Try to ensure that all pans have a good sturdy handle for safety. A good-quality non-stick pan of medium size for making béchamel sauce is useful.

You will also need oven dishes in various sizes for dishes such as lasagne; enamelled ones are good as they are attractive enough to go straight to the table for serving.

For Italian cooking it is absolutely essential, of course, to have a saucepan large enough to boil pasta in. You will need a pan that holds at least 6–7 pt (4 l) of water and has a good strong handle so that you can carry it safely to the sink to drain the pasta. There is nothing more frustrating than trying to cook pasta of any shape or form in a pan that is much too small – it won't do the pasta much good either.

Buying saucepans and other pots can be very expensive but it is worth investing in good-quality pans that will last well and give good results. Before buying take into consideration the type of heat you are using, handles, distribution and retention of heat, and also cleaning and maintenance. It is worth saving up to buy the pans you really need one at a time rather than buying a whole set of cheaper ones which look attractive but prove disappointing in use.

You may want to buy a ravioli tray for making ravioli, but it is not essential; you can use a pasta cutting wheel instead.

KNIVES AND CHOPPERS

As with pots and pans, it is worth investing in good-quality knives and cutting equipment that will last well. They are more expensive, but in the long run it pays to start with one or two decent knives rather than a whole set of knives and choppers that fall apart within a few months. A general cook's knife is absolutely essential as it can be used for most cutting or chopping jobs. A smaller vegetable knife will come in useful too. I have always found a mezzaluna of great assistance in the kitchen for chopping herbs and shredding meat; it is much easier to handle than a knife if you have never been shown how to use a knife to chop properly. I always find wooden handles easier to grip but unfortunately they cannot go in the dishwasher.

As well as the cook's knife and a smaller vegetable knife, you will find a good carving knife useful and also a long flat-bladed knife for pasta making. A knife sharpener will enable you to keep your knives really sharp.

If you are making pasta by hand, you will need a cutting wheel, which can be bought quite cheaply.

GENERAL ITEMS OF KITCHEN EQUIPMENT

1. Large colander with handles for draining vegetables and pasta

2. Salt and pepper mills

3. A few wooden spoons of various sizes

4. Several wooden or other chopping boards, one at least 15 × 20 in (38 × 51 cm) for making pasta, one that is used only for chopping onions and another for preparing fish

5. Large slotted spoon for retrieving foods from water or oil

6. Mouli-légumes or food mill

7. Splash guard for frying at high temperatures – very hot oil is likely to spit

8. Nutmeg grater and all-purpose grater

9. Mouli cheese grater (you can use an ordinary cheese grater, but the mouli grates the cheese more finely – especially important in the case of parmesan)

10. Meat beater for escalopes, etc.

11. Sieve

12. Fruit-juice press

13. Spatula

14. Long wooden rolling-pin for rolling out pasta by hand

FREEZING FOOD

Italians are not great ones for freezing food on the whole, although more and more Italians do now possess freezers.

With some foods freezing is extremely successful, however. Perhaps surprisingly, fresh pasta freezes very well, and you may find it convenient to make large quantities of several different kinds of pasta and freeze them. Most sauces also freeze well and it is a good idea to make double or triple the quantity and store some in the freezer for future use.

A NOTE ON MICROWAVES

I am the first to admit that I am not a microwave fan, though many a friend has tried to convert me. Apart from defrosting frozen food in minutes, I see little use for a microwave in the cook's kitchen. The idea seems to be that we are all too busy these days to spend hours cooking a meal, but there are so many dishes which can be cooked very quickly – and better – in the conventional ways.

THE LARDER

HERBS AND SPICES

If at all possible, all herbs should be fresh. Many herbs are very easy to grow and there are special kits available which make it even easier. Many shops and most of the main supermarkets have a good selection of fresh herbs and it should not be too difficult to find the most popular ones. If you cannot buy fresh herbs, buy a small quantity of the dried herb from a shop where they are likely to have a reasonably fast turnover of herbs or you may find that the herbs are stale, especially if they have not been stored properly. Italian cooking is based on fresh ingredients and some dishes turn out a sorrowful disappointment if the fresh herb is not used. A simple dish such as Mozzarella and Tomato Salad depends on the delicious flavour of fresh basil; dried basil has a different taste and cannot be used as a substitute here.

BASIL (*Basilico*)

Basil is probably best known, at least in Italian cooking, in *pesto* sauce, which must be made with fresh, not dried, basil. In Italy it is mostly sweet basil which is used. Although basil can be grown in Britain, it seems to be quite difficult to obtain here. The aroma of fresh basil is strong and sweet, and cries out to be used in a simmering sauce of fresh tomatoes! Basil is also used in many stews and salads. There is much argument as to whether basil should be chopped, torn, pounded or left whole; this is a matter of personal choice, although many cooks would say that the leaf should be torn and left to infuse. As well as having a pleasant scent and a delicious flavour, I am told that a pot of basil discourages wasps! – a useful tip if you are having a meal in the garden.

SAGE (*Salvia*)

Sage is very popular in Italy and although it has an unusual flavour it should be used with moderation, as it can become very overpowering. Dried sage will suffice in most recipes. In Italian cooking sage is used mainly with veal and liver, and is sometimes dropped (fresh sage only) into hot olive oil to flavour fried potatoes.

ROSEMARY (*Rosmarino*)

Rosemary has to be Italy's most popular herb. It is used in a variety of dishes including roast veal, chicken, beef and turkey, in sauces, and with vegetables and stews. Fresh rosemary has a wonderful and unforgettable aroma and should be used in whole sprigs; these are discarded before serving, as the spiky leaves can be a nuisance, especially in sauces, although you will inevitably end up with a few floating about. Rosemary is relatively easy to grow and an attractive plant; it also dries extremely well, although it does lose some of its strength and flavour when dried.

THYME (*Timo*)

Thyme is found growing wild in northern Italy but is not used a great deal in Italian cookery. When it is used, it is mainly with poultry.

BAY LEAVES (*Alloro*)

Bay leaves are used in broths, stocks, stews, soups and sauces – basically in anything that takes a considerable time to cook and, obviously, where the flavour is suitable. Bay leaves are also used when steaming fish such as salmon.

PARSLEY (*Prezzemolo*)

The flat-leaf variety of parsley seems to have much more flavour, although the curly-leaf variety is more useful for decoration. Fresh parsley is so easily available now, more so than any other herb, that there should be little or no need to use dried parsley at all. (It is also easy to grow outdoors in England.) In Italian cooking parsley is used with fish, and in stews, sauces and stuffings.

FENNEL SEEDS (*Finocchio*)

Fennel seed is mostly used in salame and is best known in flavouring Felino salame, from near Parma in northern Italy. It is also used in making sausages and, sometimes, to flavour stuffings.

MINT (*Menta*)

This is one of my favourite herbs – like rosemary it has an unforgettable aroma. I love its cool scent, which brings freshness and life to many recipes. Italians use mint sparingly in desserts and salads, and also with fish.

MARJORAM (*Maggiorana*)

Sweet marjoram is used mainly in soups and sauces, and with tomatoes. Wild marjoram (origano) is much stronger and is of course essential in Italian cooking for the distinctive flavour it gives to pizza.

GARLIC (*Aglio*)

Contrary to popular belief, Italians do not live and breathe garlic, nor do they use it in enormous quantities and in absolutely everything. In fact garlic is used carefully and is never allowed to overpower a dish. Use fresh garlic and ensure that it is crushed well. Pressed garlic purée preserved in olive oil is now available and does very well in an emergency.

SAFFRON (*Zafferano*)

Genuine saffron is expensive and is used either pounded or soaked. In Italian cooking saffron is best known for its use in Risotto Milanese.

PEPPER (*Pepe*)

A mill is essential for freshly ground black pepper. White pepper is rarely used in Italy as it has a much stronger flavour than black. If you do not have a mill do not be tempted to use that tub of pepper that has been in the back of your cupboard for years!

NUTMEG (*Noce moscata*)

I don't know what Italians would do without their nutmeg, as it is used so much and in so many dishes. It is used fresh, scraped or grated from a whole nutmeg, in stuffings, sauces such as béchamel and sweet dishes. It is also used to flavour a hot milk drink at bedtime – apparently it helps one to relax and induces sleep.

SALT (*Sale*)

Sea salt has a better flavour than ordinary table salt, but if you want to use it at table as well as in cooking you will need a salt mill. We are always being told that we should cut down on the amount of salt that we eat, but our bodies do need some salt and I feel that its flavour is essential in cooking.

YEAST (*Lievito*)

Fresh yeast will keep up to a week wrapped and refrigerated and it can also be frozen. If freezing, wrap the yeast in small packages of about an ounce each for use in the future. If you buy dried yeast keep it well wrapped and store it in a dry cupboard. There are some dried yeasts on the market now which can be added directly to the flour and they seem to work well enough. You will need to use less dried yeast – 15 g is equivalent to 30 g of fresh yeast; this quantity will be sufficient for about a kilo of flour.

FLOUR (*Farina*)

Flour used for making pasta should be from a strong hard durum wheat. Use the strong flour sold for bread-making, not normal household plain flour.

SEMOLINA (*Semolino*)

Semolina can be used in making pasta, although it is mostly commercial rather than home-made pasta that has semolina added. Buy the imported semolina flour which is available in many Italian specialist shops; English semolina is ground differently.

BREADCRUMBS (*Pane gratugiato*)

Breadcrumbs are essential for making stuffings. They must be fresh and under no circumstances should you use the kind you buy in packets that looks like bright orange sand! Bakers or specialist food shops sometimes sell fresh breadcrumbs or, failing that, simply dry out or bake some leftover bread and then grate it very finely, either on a hand grater or in a food processor.

TUNA (*Tonno*)

Tuna is another useful larder standby, as it comes in handy for lots of recipes and emergency meals. Tuna in olive oil is more expensive but it is worth it. In Italy tuna is also sold in huge tins and is bought loose in any quantity. Italians are very fussy about their tuna and will argue until the cows come home over which particular brand is superior.

ANCHOVIES (*Acciughe*)

Italians are very fond of anchovies, and use them to flavour sauces and pizza, and as a garnish. Tinned fillets of anchovy come either in brine or in olive oil. In specialist shops whole salted anchovies can be found, and these are bought loose; they must be washed thoroughly to rinse off the salt and should be left under running water for an hour or so. They should then be boned, covered with olive oil and kept refrigerated if you are not going to use them at once.

TOMATOES AND CONCENTRATED TOMATO PASTE
(*Pomidori e concentrato di pomidoro*)

It is still difficult to buy fresh imported plum tomatoes and good-quality Italian tinned plum tomatoes are the best alternative. There are many different Italian brands on the market and it is a matter of personal taste which you choose. Concentrated tomato paste can be bought either tinned or in tubes and should be used carefully because of its strength.

RICE (*Riso*)

Rice in the larder is immensely useful, especially for quick meals: if you have an onion, some rice and some stock, you have the makings of a simple risotto. Italian rice is known as Arborio; it is thicker and shorter than normal savoury rice and, unlike other types of rice, can be cooked slowly, in a small amount of liquid. When making risotto it is the only rice to use; long-grain rice cooked in this way never acquires the creamy consistency of a successful risotto.

DRIED PASTA (*Pasta asciutta*)

Dried pasta imported from Italy is usually better than the supermarket own-brands. Italians are very fussy about which brand of pasta they buy.

STOCK (*Brodo*)

Stock is used so much in Italian cooking – for soups, stews, risotto, stuffings and sauces – that it is almost essential to have some ready to hand. It is very simple to make, as you can just leave it simmering away; pour it into convenient containers or an ice-cube tray when it is done and keep it in the freezer until you need it. My cats are very fond of my stock-making days, especially when I am making chicken stock, for they know they will get a piece of chicken for themselves afterwards!

OLIVE OIL (*Olio d'oliva*)

You will certainly need to keep olive oil in the larder, as it is used extensively in Italian cooking. (See p. 34.) It is a good idea to keep two kinds of olive oil, one for general cooking and a better-quality one for salads.

ITALIAN SUN-DRIED TOMATOES (*Pomidori secchi*)

These dried tomatoes have a very distinct flavour and are delicious with cold meats, salads and salami. They are usually sold in olive oil, but can also be obtained without the oil. They are expensive, but have nevertheless become very popular.

DRIED MUSHROOMS (*Funghi secchi*)

See p. 35.

Italian Produce

Although Italian products are now more widely available than ever before in Britain, it can still be difficult to find a few of the ingredients mentioned in the recipes. In some cases it is possible to substitute another ingredient, although obviously the results will not be the same as when using the authentic ingredients. For example, if you cannot buy Parmigiano by the piece, you can use mature Cheddar instead – it tastes better and is much cheaper than the ubiquitous tubs of ready-grated parmesan. And if you cannot find a good *mozzarella* for making pizza, you can use Cheddar, Gruyère, Emmental or Fontina.

Italian tinned plum tomatoes are perfectly acceptable for making sauces when fresh tomatoes are not available or are too expensive. Tomato paste, however, in tubes or little tins, has a very strong flavour and should be used sparingly – a spoonful or so added to a sauce is enough.

Many people use unsmoked bacon where the recipe specifies *pancetta*, but the taste of bacon is quite different and I think it is a poor substitute.

Olive Oil

Italy is one of the world's greatest producers of olive oil. Olive trees are grown under widely different conditions in different parts of Italy, so obviously the oils produced from them vary considerably in flavour. Tuscan oil, for example, is stronger and heavier, both in colour and in flavour, than the oil from nearby Liguria.

There are so many different olive oils available now in Britain that it can be difficult to decide which to buy. Some olive oils are labelled 'cold-pressed', which means that the olives are stoned and the oil extracted without the use of heat, usually by putting them through a hydraulic press. This oil is made from the very best olives and has no solvents or chemicals added to it; it has a distinctive green colour. It is the oil to use for salads or in a special sauce.

When refined olive oils, including 'virgin' oils, are extracted, however, the temperature is raised to 60–90°C during pressing in order to extract more oil. Oils which are pressed under heat are much less green in colour, more a pale yellow, and have less flavour. They are also less expensive than cold-pressed oils and can be used in general cooking. Try to experiment with a few oils to give you some idea of the different flavours and strengths. Keep oil in a dark, cool cupboard in the bottle you bought it in. Never keep olive oil in the fridge. If the weather is very cold your olive oil may go cloudy, but the cloudiness will disappear once the oil becomes warmer.

Most of us are now aware that vegetable oil is much better for us than animal fat. (Italians have one of the lowest rates of heart disease in Europe.) Olive oil is a monounsaturated oil and contains no cholesterol. It is very easily digested and absorbed by the body. It is particularly good for cooking as it does not undergo the same deterioration as other vegetable oils when it is heated.

However, if you do not like the taste of olive oil you can substitute a good vegetable oil in some of the recipes – but never use anything but olive oil in salad dressing or mayonnaise.

FUNGHI SECCHI

Italians, as you may know, absolutely rave about their wild mushrooms and will spend hours or even days hunting the woods for them. It is necessary to leave very early in the morning, if possible just after it has rained, and you must be prepared for a very long and rough trek.

You will often see mushrooms of different kinds being sold in Italian markets, spread out in their huge baskets, drying in the sun.

The most sought after of the many varieties of wild mushrooms found in Italy are *porcini* (*Botulus edulis*), which can be bought, dried, in Britain too. They also grow wild in Britain, but if you do pick wild mushrooms, make sure that you are armed with a reliable book or go accompanied by an expert, so that you know exactly what you are picking.

If you ever have the good fortune to eat fresh *porcini* – sliced, dipped in egg yolk, lightly covered in fresh breadcrumbs and fried in the very best olive oil – you will never forget their flavour and their wonderful aroma. In autumn, when we have had a few days of damp weather, the men of our family often go out hunting for these mushrooms, of which we are excessively fond. They return with large quantities of them, and then sit around in the warm kitchen, which once belonged to my husband's grandparents, waiting while Zia Antonia prepares the mushrooms and relating in great detail how they managed to find so many excellent ones.

Dried *porcini* are also delicious; they are very expensive, but you only need a small quantity to transform a dish. Always save the water in which they have been cooked, as this contains much of the flavour.

Do not use them as you would use ordinary mushrooms – they are a delicacy and should be treated as such.

MEAT PRODUCTS

PARMA HAM (*Prosciutto crudo*)

Parma ham is a cured ham produced in Piedmont, Lombardy, Emilia-Romagna and Veneto; it is not, as many people-believe, a smoked ham. The producers are controlled by a consortium which lays down strict requirements regarding the methods of production. When all the requirements are met, a mark looking like a crown is branded on to the ham; only ham so marked is genuine Parma ham.

I recently visited the Lunardini factory at Collechio where Parma ham has been produced for over a hundred years, and watched the ham being made. Fresh pork rumps arrive at the factory already cut into the familiar shape. The joints are then salted and put into freezers for one week at 4°C above freezing. After a week the salt is blown off and the joint massaged, re-salted and frozen again at 2°C. After this stage comes the 'rest period', where the top layer of salt is blown off and the joints are stored for between forty and fifty days at 0°C. Once the rest period is over the joints are hung to dry for a week or ten days and then any cracks are covered with fat to stop the air penetrating. A second layer of fat is applied during this hanging stage. By this time the hams will be six months old.

The joints remain in the same storage area for another six months. At one year old they will have reached their required maturity and each ham must weigh at least seven kilos.

I was informed by Signor Rossi, the owner of the factory, that the province of Parma alone produces around six million hams a year of which 18–20 per cent are exported.

Parma ham is delicious, but expensive, so when buying take care to ensure that the ham is sliced very finely and laid out flat. Although the long slices may look more attractive the smaller slices are sometimes sweeter and tastier. Eat the ham as soon as possible. It should never be served chilled, straight from the refrigerator.

Some shops will sell the end piece from the ham at reduced price; this is excellent for making a stock, broth or soup.

Parma ham should not be confused with a ham called San Daniele – also delicious – which is produced around Venice.

SALAME

Italy has so many different kinds of salame it would be impossible to list all of them. Salame is made all over the country and the flavour, shape, size, saltiness and maturity vary from locality to locality.

Most salame in Italy now is made on an industrial scale but many firms try to follow the traditional methods and recipes.

Salame di Felino comes from Felino outside Parma and is one of the best in Italy. It is imported into this country and is usually excellent. It tends to look more home-made than salame such as Milano, and has a more delicate flavour. It is made from pure pork and the fat content is about 18–20 per cent. It is flavoured with whole peppercorns. Felino salame is best eaten relatively young; it is one of the most expensive salame you will come across but it is worth every penny.

Milano is a much fatter-looking salame than Felino. It is made from a mixture of pork and beef and has a sharper flavour than Felino. Most delicatessens stock this and it is probably Italy's best-known and most widely exported salame.

Genovese salame is also well known – it is slightly leaner than Milano, with larger, more visible pieces of fat. It is made from pork and *vitellone* (young cow) and has a good strong flavour and aroma.

Various strong, highly spiced types of Italian salame are sold in this country – the best-known is Napoletano, which is made from pork and beef. There is also Mugnano, from the south, which is highly spiced with red pepper, and Ventricina, another highly spiced salame.

You may also come across salame described as '*casalingo*', which is made from a beef and pork mixture and comes from various parts of Italy. This type of salame is usually relatively mild in flavour.

When you buy salame, try and buy a single large piece or even a whole sausage; there are many '*cacciatori*' – small salame – available. If you buy salame which is already sliced and do not eat it the same day it will quickly dry out. Whole salami or large pieces need not be refrigerated – they can be stored for a short time in a cool, dry place wrapped in a cloth. To slice salame you need a longish knife which is nice and sharp. Hold the salame firmly with one hand, keeping your thumb well out of the way of the knife, and slice diagonally.

BRESAOLA

Bresaola, which comes from Lombardy, is beef fillet cured in salt and then air-dried. It is eaten sliced very thinly as an *antipasto*. Once sliced – and this really needs to be done on a machine – it should be eaten quickly. Lay out the Bresaola, coat very lightly with a good-flavoured olive oil, sprinkle lightly with fresh lemon juice and grind some black pepper over it. Some people compare Bresaola to *prosciutto*; I find its flavour completely different, although equally delicious.

MORTADELLA

Mortadella is a sausage from Bologna, made in various sizes, from very small baby ones to huge sausages weighing up to 100 kg. These giant ones are usually made only for special occasions, however. Most good Italian grocers will sell the traditional type of *mortadella*, weighing about 8 kg. *Mortadella* can be made from a mixture of pork and liver or pork and beef, but the traditional *mortadella* is pure pork.

Mortadella should be very finely sliced and eaten in an *antipasto* of mixed meats or in sandwiches; it is also used in cooking. Be sure that you buy Bologna *mortadella*, as any other kind may be disappointing or worse.

PANCETTA

Pancetta, another pork product, looks like a large fatty salame. The pork is cured and spiced and then rolled up into a salame shape. It is not smoked as many people think, and it is not bacon – in fact it has a totally different flavour from bacon.

The quality of *pancetta* varies considerably from the quite attractive, leanish-looking *pancetta* to a cheaper kind which has a lot of rolled fat. You can buy *pancetta* thinly sliced or you can get it in one thick slice if you are going to chop it up for cooking. *Pancetta* can be kept in the freezer if you find it convenient to buy more than you need to use immediately.

Good-quality *pancetta* can be eaten raw, finely sliced; it is also used for numerous other dishes such as soups, stews and stuffings, and of course it is essential in Spaghetti alla Carbonara.

COPPA

Coppa is a cured pork product, made from the shoulder (*spalla*). It is much leaner than *pancetta*, with a more delicate and distinctive flavour, and is much more expensive. It is usually eaten as an *antipasto* and is sometimes used in cooking, but its flavour is best raw. There is another similar cured meat from the shoulder called *culatello*, which is absolutely delicious but very, very expensive and still quite difficult to get hold of in Britain; should you come across it, it is well worth a try.

COTECHINO AND ZAMPONE

You may have seen these hanging in Italian shops and wondered what to do with them. Both are made from pork and are specialities of the province of Emilia-Romagna. *Zampone* is a kind of raw salame, a pork mixture which is stuffed into the skin of a pig's trotter and is then soaked in brine to preserve the meat and give it its characteristic flavour. *Cotechino* looks like a big salame and is delicious cooked in sauce (see p. 182).

ITALIAN CHEESES

Obviously it pays when buying cheese to go to a reputable establishment that has a high turnover and a good knowledge of cheeses. This is even more important when the shop has a large selection. Many such shops are now very willing to let you taste a few cheeses and to offer advice on storing the cheese. Cheese (with the exception, perhaps, of small amounts of grated Parmigiano if you don't have any other option) should never be frozen and should be consumed as quickly as possible. If the weather is not too hot, cheese keeps better if it is not in the fridge. The ideal storage place is a cool larder but, as few people now have larders, the salad tray of the fridge will do. Try to avoid wrapping cheese in clingfilm – use greaseproof paper, foil or even a clean dry cloth for hard cheeses. Lastly, do not buy more than you need and if you are experimenting with new cheeses don't be tempted to buy too many different types at once.

As well as parmesan, Gorgonzola, Bel Paese and Dolce Latte, renowned throughout the world, Italy produces other less well known cheeses such as Toscanello, and many locally made cheeses which are rarely exported. I have listed some of the more easily obtainable ones, with a brief description of each to help you choose when buying.

PARMESAN

Parmigiano, or parmesan as it is called in Britain, is one of the world's great cheeses, and its flavour is essential to many Italian dishes; it is used in cooking, it is eaten on its own at the end of a meal, with a glass of red wine, and grated Parmigiano is served with most pasta dishes.

I have sometimes heard this superb cheese described as 'smelly, sickly and overpowering', but a true Parmigiano has a distinctive rich flavour and is never harsh or overstrong; I suppose that what is being referred to is the foul-smelling sawdust which is sold in plastic tubs as 'parmesan'. Unfortunately this product detracts from the reputation of the true Parmigiano, and is an insult to the expertise, developed through the centuries, of Italian cheesemakers.

The making of Parmigiano-Reggiano – the true parmesan – and other *grana* cheeses, also loosely known as parmesan, is strictly controlled by Italian law. '*Grana*', meaning 'of grains', is the name given to all the finely grained hard cheeses originating in the Po valley in northern Italy; Parmigiano-Reggiano is the finest of these, being matured for up to four years. *Grana* cheese is thought to have been produced as early as 1150; it seems likely that it was made in the first instance because there was an abundance of fresh milk and it was useful to be able to make it into a product which could be preserved and consumed in the future.

Grana cheese is controlled by a consortium, established in 1957, which grants seals of quality showing that the cheeses have reached a recognized standard and have been made with milk from the designated production areas, known as '*zone tipica*'. Parmigiano-Reggiano is produced with milk from the provinces of Parma, Modena and Mantua on the right bank of the Po, and Reggio-Emilia and Bologna on the left bank of the Reno; Grana Padano is produced in the Po valley area, more specifically from the provinces of Cremona, Piacenza, Brescia, Bergamo, Pavia, Alessandria, Asti, Cuneo, Novara, Vercelli, Torino, Milan, Como, Sondrio, Trento, Padua (Padova), Varese, Venice, Verona, Rovigo, Treviso, Vicenza and Mantua (Mantova) on the left bank of the Po, Bologna on the right bank of the Reno river, and Ravenna, Ferrara and Forli.

A whole Parmigiano cheese is very impressive, in size, weight and colour, and each cheese is stamped with various markings and seals granted by the consortium, showing that the traditional methods of cheese-making have been followed and guaranteeing the authenticity of the cheese.

I was recently lucky enough to be invited to watch the making of Parmigiano-Reggiano at Collechio by the Lunardini family, who have been making it for over a century, and also of Grana Padano at Signor Romanini's, just outside Piacenza.

The cheese is made from partly skimmed unpasteurized milk. The cows are milked in the evening and then again in the morning, and the evening milk is allowed to stand so that the cream will rise and can be skimmed off. (It is used to make butter.) The skimmed milk is then mixed with the unskimmed morning milk in huge copper vats. These have a double inner lining containing tubes through which hot steam can be passed. This heats the milk gradually to 28°C; when it has reached this temperature, rennet is added. The machine is then switched off and the milk left to coagulate for approximately fifteen minutes. While we were waiting I asked how much milk was needed to make one 40 kg cheese – the answer was 550 kg! After fifteen minutes the curd is broken up into small grains with a *spino*, a tool fitted to the copper vat. The curd is heated to 45°C, and is then lifted out of the vat on to a cheesecloth by two people with long poles, leaving the whey behind in the vat. (When I was there the leftover whey was being used to make *ricotta* cheese.) The curd is pressed into a mould – each copper vat contains enough milk to make a single cheese – and is left for one day. Then it is put into brine and remains there for twenty days. The cheese will lose 20 per cent of its weight between the time that it is first made and the time when it is finally ready to eat. After twenty days the cheese is lifted out of its salt bath and is stored for at least a year, but no longer than four.

Grana Padano, also loosely known as parmesan, is matured for between one and two years and should weigh at least 24 kg at the end of its maturation period.

When the cheese is finally cut open it should have tiny traces of moisture on the surface – this shows that perfection has been attained, and the cheesemaker is relieved and proud that his cheese has passed its test.

Cheeses are sold at four stages over the maturation period –

up to four years in the case of Parmigiano-Reggiano – and these are:

Giovanne	young, just after one year old
Vecchio	old, usually two years old
Stravecchio	mature, over three years old
Stravecchione	very mature, four years old.

When buying Parmigiano check that it is genuine by looking for the official markings on the outside of the cheese. If it does not have these markings and seals then it is not a genuine Parmigiano which has reached the standards required by the consortium. It is also important to buy from a reputable firm which has experience in buying, selling, storing and cutting the cheese. Try and buy from a shop where the cheese is cut as required from a whole cheese and where there is a good turnover, otherwise you could end up with a piece that has been sitting wrapped in clingfilm in the fridge for days on end. The art of cutting a whole Parmigiano cheese takes months to acquire. A short-bladed, leaf-shaped knife is used to score and prise open the cheese, which is then cut into smaller pieces for selling. Do not be tempted to buy a lot more than you actually need, as the fresher the cheese the better. Once you get your bit of Parmigiano home wrap it in a clean dry cloth or greaseproof paper, and store it if possible in a cool larder or cupboard. Try and keep it out of the fridge, and if you do have to put it in the fridge place it in the least cold place and take it out at least an hour before you are going to eat it. If a mould appears, simply scrape it away lightly with a knife.

Both Padano and Parmigiano-Reggiano are good eating cheeses; Padano is the one to buy for grating. Parmigiano-Reggiano is very expensive, and should be eaten on its own, sliced very finely so that the taste can be savoured. Once you have grated Parmigiano it will dry out much more quickly but it will still keep for a few weeks in the fridge – or it can be frozen, though this is not ideal.

Parmigiano has a wonderful distinctive and delicate flavour, and does not have an unpleasant smell at all. It is a straw-yellow colour and the texture is very fine-grained with hardly any eyes (holes).

The Markings on a Grana Padano

a.   b.   c.

a. *The seal of quality*

This marking is branded on to the cheese by the consortium and indicates that the cheese has reached the required standard of quality and flavour. Without this marking the cheese cannot be classified as Grana Padano.

b. *The provisional seal*

This mark indicates the place of origin of the cheese. This is affixed by the cheesemaker.

c. *Grana Padano wording on the flank (side)*

This mark is made after the seal of quality; it is mostly for the benefit of the public, as it enables the cheese to be identified after it has been cut.

The Markings on a Grana Padano

ASIAGO

This cheese is now made from cows' milk, but originally it was made with ewes' milk. It is firm, granular and yellow, with a hard golden rind. It is usually ripened for about six months and has a sharp flavour.

BEL PAESE

Bel paese means literally 'beautiful country'. This cheese was created by Egidio Galbani in 1906. The wrapping of the cheese has a map of Italy on the front and also a picture of Abbot Antonio Stoppani, a friend of the Galbani family. Bel Paese is sweet, with a smooth yet slightly plastic texture, and is produced in huge quantities by Galbani, a major exporter of Italian produce. It can be used in cooking and also comes in the form of a cheese spread, in individual portions.

BURRINI

You will see these small pear-shaped cheeses from southern Italy hanging from the ceiling in most Italian specialist shops. There is a knob of butter at the centre of the cheese – hence the name – and the taste is fairly mild. The cheeses are sometimes dipped in wax to preserve them. *Burrini* are usually eaten after they have been ripening for a few weeks.

CACIOTTA

Caciotta were originally small cheeses produced locally, and from any kind of milk, but now they are mostly made in factories from cows' milk. When made by the farmers themselves in the traditional way the cheese varies greatly both in shape and in flavour; it is a semi-soft cheese with a creamy texture, and is white to pale yellow in colour. The flavour may be sweet and mild or quite sharp – if you try *caciotta* in different regions of Italy you will realize how much it can vary. It is definitely worth trying, as it has a fresh, home-produced flavour of its own.

CAPRINI

Caprini are made from goats' milk (*capra* means 'goat' in Italian); it can be difficult to find these mild but distinctively flavoured cheeses.

DOLCE LATTE

This cheese is widely available in Britain. 'Dolce Latte' ('sweet milk') is a registered trade mark. The cheese is commercially produced in factories using cows' milk; it is blue-veined, smooth and creamy, and the flavour is quite mild.

FONTAL

Fontal is very similar to Fontina (see below); in fact it was known as Fontina until 1951, when it was decided at the Stresa Convention that the name Fontina should be reserved for cheese made in the Val d'Aosta. Unlike Fontina, Fontal is made from pasteurized milk; it has a darker rind than Fontina, and is mass-produced in Lombardy and Piedmont.

FONTINA

Fontina is now quite well known in Britain. It can be used in cooking, but it is also a delicious table cheese. It is made from unpasteurized cows' milk in the Val d'Aosta in the Italian Alps. It has a delicate flavour, very slightly nutty, and the texture is smooth and slightly elastic, with a few small holes.

FORMAGGINI (*small cheeses*)

Formaggini means small, locally made cheeses, but in practice it usually refers to cheese spreads or small processed cheeses.

GORGONZOLA

This is Italy's foremost blue-veined cheese. It has a sharp flavour from the green-blue veins which contrasts wonderfully with the delicate paste of the rest of the cheese. Originally Gorgonzola, which comes from Lombardy, was made only in the winter months; it is now made throughout the year, but no longer at Gorgonzola itself. It is sold wrapped in foil. Although Gorgonzola is sharp in taste it should not have a strong, unpleasant or bitter flavour. The cheese is matured for approximately three or four months. There is also a white, unveined Gorgonzola Bianco, sometimes known as 'Pannerare', which is extremely difficult to find.

MASCARPONE

This is a delicious cream cheese; once tasted, its velvety texture and mild, slightly sweet flavour is never forgotten. In Italy it is produced all year round and is usually exported and sold in plastic tubs. It should be eaten as soon as possible and is used extensively in cooking, especially for desserts (see pp. 241 and 245).

MOZZARELLA

Mozzarella imported fresh from Italy has a mild, delicate flavour. Unfortunately, much of the *mozzarella* sold in Britain is factory made and has absolutely no taste or flavour; often it is not even made in Italy. If you are ever lucky enough to find it, do try the delicious *mozzarella di bufala* – it is made from buffalo milk and has a much more distinctive and fresher flavour than cows' milk *mozzarella*.

PARMIGIANO-REGGIANO

See p. 41.

PECORINO

Pecorino comes from the Italian word *pecora*, meaning sheep, as this cheese is made from ewes' milk. It varies considerably throughout Italy; it is a semi-hard cheese, drum-shaped, with a hard rind. If you can find a good one it will be one of the finest Italian cheeses you will taste. Generally those made in the south have a much stronger flavour.

PECORINO ROMANO

Much stronger and drier than a normal *pecorino*, as it is matured for at least eight months and is controlled by the Stresa Convention of 1951, which defined particular areas of cheese production. It can be grated and sprinkled over pasta and soups, as well as being eaten on its own.

PECORINO SARDO

This is a traditional Sardinian cheese, also made from ewes' milk in much the same way as Pecorino Romano. It is stronger than a normal *pecorino*.

PROVOLONE

Provolone is now quite well known in Britain and has become popular, as some very good Provolone is now imported. Originally Provolone was made in the south but is now widely produced in the Po valley area; it is made from cows' milk and sold in various shapes and sizes up to 30–35 kg. It is also sometimes smoked. It is used in cooking and is delicious as a table cheese served with pears.

RICOTTA

Ricotta is a mild soft cheese, traditionally made from whey. In Britain we can buy imported *ricotta*, but it is also made in this country as it has a very short life. Used extensively in Italian cooking for stuffings in pasta, sweet puddings and cakes, or mixed with fresh herbs.

SAN GAUDENZIO

This is an extremely popular cheese in Britain. It is also known as *torta*, which means 'cake' in Italian, as the cheese is made from layers of Gorgonzola and *mascarpone* and looks, and is, even more delicious than a cream gâteau!

STRACCHINO

This is a very soft, even runny cheese from Lombardy and needs to be eaten quickly! It has a mild, creamy flavour and deserves to be better known in Britain.

TALEGGIO

Taleggio is a soft, mild cheese and has a greyish rind, which is not meant to be eaten. It is named after a town near Bergamo. A good table cheese that appeals to most people.

ITALIAN COFFEE

In Italy espresso coffee is served everywhere, very strong, in very small cups. It is drunk at any time of the day. Cappuccino, which comes in a normal-sized cup, is espresso coffee topped up with frothy milk. For breakfast, many Italians drink *caffe latte* – espresso coffee with milk.

If you want to make your own Italian coffee you will need

the special coffee-pot for making it. There are two types, the Moka and the Napoletana, and both work on the same principle, heating the water in one chamber and filtering it through finely ground coffee into a second chamber for pouring. If you buy a pot in Britain it will no doubt have instructions telling you how to make the coffee. If you buy one in Italy, however – they are cheaper there – there may not be any accompanying instructions, so I have given a brief description of how to use them.

First you will need some good Italian roasted coffee, which must be very finely ground. Many home grinders do not make a good job of this, so either get your local delicatessen or coffee suppliers to grind it for you or buy some ready packed Italian espresso coffee – many reputable Italian brands are imported into Britain.

La Napoletana

The coffee-pot will divide into four parts. Fill the bottom part (without the spout) with fresh cold water up to the little hole near the top. Push in the filter part and fill it with coffee. Don't press the coffee down and don't be mean with it – you need to have a nice mound. Now screw on the filter top and over it the part with the spout on top (the spout will be upside down).

Put the pot carefully on the heat (you may need to buy a smaller ring attachment if you are using gas, to prevent the pot from falling over). Leave it on the heat until steam appears and then turn the pot over so that the spout is now the right way up. (Your first attempts should be done over the sink.) Leave the water to filter through the coffee into the lower part of the pot. It may sound as if it will take all morning to make the coffee, but it doesn't!

Do not reheat coffee. Try to use it all at once or save it for cooking purposes.

La Moka

This method produces the coffee rather more quickly and makes slightly stronger, thicker coffee.

The pot comes in three parts. Fill the bottom part up to the safety valve with fresh cold water. Place the metal filter on top and fill it generously with coffee as with La Napoletana. Screw the top of the pot on tightly and put the pot on the heat as with La Napoletana. After a short time you will hear the water starting to rise up through the coffee into the upper part; when this happens turn the heat down. Eventually you will hear a spluttering sound, which indicates that all the water has filtered through. The coffee is now ready.

WEIGHING AND MEASURING

Specific weights and measures are given in the recipes in this book, but in Italy scales and measuring jugs are rarely used in home cooking. Most people learn to cook by watching others and they know from experience exactly how much of an ingredient is needed. At first this may seem rather haphazard – how can anyone make pasta without even looking at the scales? – but you will find, after making a few tries and gaining a little confidence, that it works very well. You will soon learn how many eggs you need to bind the amount of flour you are using, and you will get to know from the feel of it when the pasta dough is ready for rolling. And with practice you will find that this way of cooking without exact measurements is not only quicker but much more enjoyable too.

When you are following these recipes, remember that the weights and measurements are there for your guidance only. Tastes differ as to how much seasoning, herbs or spices should be used, and you may want to adjust the quantities to suit yourself.

THE RECIPES

STOCK AND SOUP

BRODO
Chicken Stock

Chicken stock is one of the most useful things to keep in your fridge or freezer; it can be used on its own or with rice or pasta to make soup, and with Arborio rice to make risotto. The vegetables can be varied according to what is available.

2 CARROTS	APPROX. 2 LB (0.9 KG)
2 RIPE TOMATOES	CHICKEN MEAT AND BONES
1 MEDIUM ONION	SALT AND PEPPER
2 STICKS OF CELERY	1 TABLESPOON OLIVE OIL

1. Peel the carrots and skin the onion.
2. Chop all the vegetables roughly.
3. Put the vegetables, meat and bones into a large saucepan and pour over approximately 2 pt (1.1 l) water. Add the seasoning and olive oil, bring to the boil and simmer gently for 2 hours.

If it is not to be used immediately, allow to cool, strain, pour into an ice-cube tray or other container and freeze.

BRODO DI VITELLO
Veal Stock

1 MEDIUM–SIZED ONION
2 CARROTS
1 STICK CELERY
$1\frac{1}{2}$ (0.7 KG) LB VEAL AND BONES
SALT AND FRESHLY GROUND BLACK PEPPER
2 TABLESPOONS OLIVE OIL

1. Clean and roughly chop the vegetables.
2. Put everything into a large saucepan with 2 pt (1.1 l) water, bring to the boil and then simmer for at least $1\frac{1}{2}$ hours.
3. Strain and cool. Use within a couple of days or freeze in small tubs or in an ice-cube tray.

NB. The same method can be used to make beef or pork stock.

ZUPPA DI POMIDORO
Tomato Soup

This is a beautiful light summer soup. You can add herbs to vary the flavour; fresh basil is particularly good.

2 LB (0.9 KG) RIPE PLUM TOMATOES
$1\frac{3}{4}$ PT (2 L) CHICKEN OR VEGETABLE STOCK
SALT AND FRESHLY GROUND BLACK PEPPER
I TABLESPOON ARBORIO RICE

1. Wash and chop the tomatoes. Put them into a medium pan with half the stock and the seasoning, bring to the boil and simmer for 10 minutes.
2. Add the rice and the remainder of the stock and simmer for a further 20 minutes.
3. Sieve or liquidize and serve.

MINESTRA

Don't get this mixed up with minestrone, which is basically a vegetable soup. Minestra is a clear broth made from a good stock with either pasta or rice in it. It appears on most restaurant menus as a first course; it is the staple diet of the elderly and anyone who is feeling delicate.

2 TOMATOES	HALF A CHICKEN
1 LEEK	1 TEASPOON OIL
1 ONION	SALT AND PEPPER
2 CARROTS	SMALL PASTA SHAPES OR
	SPAGHETTI BROKEN UP

1. Clean the vegetables and cut in large pieces.
2. Wash the chicken and cut into about 4 pieces.
3. Fill a large saucepan three-quarters full of water, bring to the boil and add all the ingredients apart from the pasta. Season, and simmer for at least 1 hour.
4. Drain through a sieve (the chicken meat can be eaten separately), put the stock back into the pan and add some small pasta shapes. Cook for about 5–8 minutes, or as directed on the packet.

MINESTRONE

Minestrone is basically a vegetable soup, but it is usually made with meat stock. Here I give a few different recipes; no doubt in time you will develop your own favourites by ringing the changes on the vegetables.

I MEDIUM ONION	2 STICKS CELERY
I LEEK	2 TOMATOES
HALF A BULB OF FENNEL	3 TABLESPOONS OLIVE OIL
I LB (450 G) POTATOES	SALT AND PEPPER
2 LARGE OR 3 MEDIUM CARROTS	2 PT (1.1 L) CHICKEN, BEEF OR VEGETABLE STOCK

1. Wash, peel and prepare all the vegetables. Decide what sort of size you want them to be – *minestrones* vary considerably – and chop them accordingly, with a food processor if you have one.

2 Heat the olive oil in a large saucepan. Add the chopped vegetables, starting with the onion and leek, then the fennel and finally all the rest. Let them cook for a couple of minutes. Season.

3. Add the stock and bring to the boil. Turn down the heat and simmer for at least 1 hour.

MINESTRONE WITH PASTA SHAPES

This minestrone has pasta shapes added and the vegetables should not be cut too small. It is a substantial soup, good in winter.

I MEDIUM ONION
I LB (450 G) POTATOES
I PARSNIP
2 LARGE CARROTS
I STICK CELERY
I LEEK
2 TOMATOES
FEW GREEN BEANS

HANDFUL OF CABBAGE OR
    SPINACH
OLIVE OIL
SEASONING
2½ PT (1.4 L) CHICKEN, BEEF
    OR VEGETABLE BROTH
PASTA SHAPES

1. Prepare the vegetables. The cabbage or spinach should be shredded and the green beans cut into ¼ inch (1 cm) pieces. (The food processor will do this.)
2. Heat the oil in a large saucepan. Add the onion and then gradually all the other vegetables starting with the hardest and ending with the cabbage or spinach. Cook for a few minutes. Season.
3. Add the stock, bring to the boil and then simmer for at least 1 hour.
4. When it is nearly ready the soup can either be left as it is and the pasta shapes added, or it can be liquidized a little and the pasta cooked in it. Choose smallish pasta such as short macaroni and cook in the soup for as long as directed on the packet.

MINESTRONE CON FAGIOLI
Bean Minestrone

I like to cook this on a cold winter day, as it is quite a substantial soup and only needs something light to follow it to make a satisfying meal.

3 OZ (85 G) DRIED BORLOTTI
   BEANS
1 MEDIUM ONION
1 PARSNIP
2 MEDIUM-SIZED POTATOES
1 STICK CELERY
2 CARROTS
A HANDFUL OF CABBAGE
3 RIPE TOMATOES
1 TABLESPOON CHOPPED
   PARSLEY
1 OZ (30 G) BUTTER
OLIVE OIL
SALT AND FRESHLY GROUND
   BLACK PEPPER
2 PT (1.1 L) CHICKEN OR
   VEGETABLE STOCK

1. Soak the beans overnight. Boil for 20 minutes and drain.
2. Now follow recipe for Minestrone 2, adding the beans 30 minutes before the end of the cooking time.

This minestrone should be coarse and doesn't need to be liquidized.

BEAN AND CABBAGE SOUP

Bean and cabbage soup may sound like a punishment, but in fact it is very pleasant and filling.

1 OZ (30 G) BORLOTTI BEANS
1 OZ (30 G) CANNELLINI
  BEANS
1 OZ (30 G) FLAGEOLET BEANS
1 OZ (30 G) BUTTER BEANS OR
  LIMA BEANS

1 LARGE GREEN CABBAGE
½ OZ (30 G) BUTTER
2 TABLESPOONS OLIVE OIL
1 CLOVE OF GARLIC, CRUSHED
2 PT (1.1 L) VEGETABLE STOCK
SALT AND PEPPER

1. Soak the beans overnight. Boil for 20 minutes and drain.
2. Wash and shred the cabbage.
3. In a large pan, melt the butter and add the oil and crushed garlic. When the garlic has cooked a little, add the beans and cabbage and cook for 5 minutes.
4. Add the stock, bring to the boil and season. Simmer for 30 minutes or until sufficiently reduced.
5. Liquidize if desired.

Lentil Soup

If you like, potatoes can be added to this recipe to make a more hearty soup.

1 LARGE ONION	SALT AND FRESHLY GROUND
1 OZ (30 G) BUTTER	BLACK PEPPER
2 TABLESPOONS OLIVE OIL	1½ PT (0.9 L) VEGETABLE OR
1 CLOVE OF GARLIC	CHICKEN STOCK
4 OZ (115 G) LENTILS	1 TABLESPOON LEMON JUICE

1. Peel and chop the onion finely.
2. Melt the butter in a medium-sized pan. Add the oil, crushed garlic, onion and lentils. Cook for 2 minutes. Season.
3. Pour in the stock, bring to the boil and then simmer for 30 minutes.
4. Liquidize or sieve, add the lemon juice, check the seasoning and serve.

PASSATELLI

To make *passatelli*, a mixture of breadcrumbs, parmesan cheese and egg is pressed through the largest holes of a mouli-légumes and cooked in stock.

To serve 4

1½ PT (0.9 L) STOCK
2 OZ (55 G) FRESHLY GRATED PARMESAN
1½ OZ (45 G) FRESH BREADCRUMBS
NUTMEG
1 EGG

1. Prepare the stock, bringing it to a slow boil.
2. In the meantime mix the parmesan, breadcrumbs and nutmeg together either on a large board, making a well in the centre, or in a large mixing bowl. Add the egg to the parmesan and breadcrumbs, and knead together well.
3. When your stock is ready and at boiling point, press the mixture through the mouli-légumes (use the disc with the largest holes) straight into the broth. Boil gently for about 2 minutes, and then turn off the heat and leave it for another 3 minutes or so. Serve immediately.

ANTIPASTI

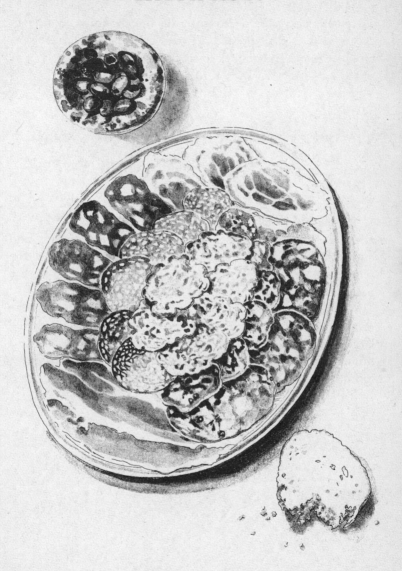

ANTIPASTO MISTO
Mixed Antipasto

This can look extremely attractive if it is nicely arranged on a large oval serving plate. I have suggested a suitable selection of meats, but you can vary them according to preference. All the meat should be fresh and of the best quality. Lots of continental food shops will weigh up a mixture for you. Make sure that there is plenty for everyone.

To serve 4

8 SLICES PARMA HAM
4 SLICES *COPPA*
4 SLICES *MORTADELLA*
8 SLICES FELINO SALAME
8 SLICES NEAPOLITAN OR
   OTHER SPICY SALAME

SMALL DISHES OF ASSORTED
OLIVES, ARTICHOKE HEARTS
IN OIL, *PORCINI*
MUSHROOMS IN OIL,
ITALIAN MIXED PICKLES IN
OIL
SUN–DRIED TOMATOES

Place the meats neatly and attractively on a large oval plate, the largest slices on the outside and the smallest in the middle.

Serve with fresh crusty bread and a good full-bodied red wine. Pasta with a plain tomato sauce goes well after mixed antipasto.

PROSCIUTTO CRUDO CON MELONE
Parma Ham and Melon

Unfortunately, Parma ham is expensive, but this is a superb dish for a special occasion. It is served as an *antipasto* all over Italy. Use good-quality Parma ham and make sure that there is enough – depending on the size of the slices, you should allow three or four slices for each person.

Presentation is important: the ham can be arranged either on a large serving platter or on individual plates, and each slice of ham should be laid out separately – never have them layered on top of each other. The ham should have been sliced very thinly in the shop where you bought it and packed with a sheet of paper between each layer; when you want to transfer it to a plate for serving, curl each slice gently round a fork and lay it on the plate.

The melon should be on a separate plate; use a ripe, sweet melon – Charentais or cantaloup – and cut it into boat shapes. I find it works better if you allow your guests to discard their own melon rind rather than removing it for them beforehand.

Serve some fresh crusty bread and a good hearty red wine with the ham. A pasta dish with tomato sauce would go well afterwards.

Parma ham can also be served with fresh ripe figs, or with a selection of other cold meats, olives and pickles.

MUSSELS

Mussels are sold live and their shells should be closed. Any whose shells are open should be tapped and if they remain open they should be discarded. You will see that each mussel has a bunch of hairs attached to the shell; this is called the beard and it should be pulled away. Scrub the mussels under cold water and then place them in a pan of clean salted water until you are ready to use them. Boil them in water until they open, and discard any that remain closed.

The cleaning and preparation of mussels is not so much of a chore as you might think; it is quite quickly done once you get started, and is well worth while.

STUFFED MUSSELS

When we are staying in Italy we often go down to the coast and eat at one of the excellent restaurants serving fresh fish. We first had these stuffed mussels at a restaurant in the little seaside and fishing town of Lerici.

APPPROX. 10 MUSSELS PER
    PERSON
2 SHALLOTS
2 TABLESPOONS FRESH PARSLEY
4 OZ (115 G) SOFTENED
    BUTTER
2 CLOVES OF GARLIC, CRUSHED

1 TABLESPOON FRESH
    BREADCRUMBS
2 TABLESPOONS DRY WHITE
    WINE
SALT AND FRESHLY GROUND
    BLACK PEPPER

1. Clean the mussels and boil them as directed on page 73. Open each shell at the hinge with a knife and discard the empty half.
2. Chop the shallots and parsley finely and mix with the butter, garlic and breadcrumbs. Add the wine and seasoning. (This can be done in a food processor.)
3. Place all the mussels in their shells on a baking tray, put a spoonful of the mixture over each mussel, and cook in the oven at Mark 6 (400°F, 200°C) for about 5 minutes.

The amounts given will make enough stuffing for 40-60 mussels.

ACCIUGHE FRITTA
Fried Anchovies

To serve 4

1½ LB (0.7 KG) FRESH ANCHOVIES
PLAIN FLOUR
½ PT (275 ML) OLIVE OIL
LEMON JUICE
FRESH PARSLEY, FINELY CHOPPED

1. Prepare the anchovies by removing the heads and gutting
– cutting each fish from the belly to the tail and gently pulling
out the inside. Wash and dry with kitchen paper.
2. Have enough plain flour ready on a plate to coat the fish.
Dip the anchovies into the flour and shake gently.
3. In a large shallow frying-pan heat the olive oil until very hot
and then add the anchovies a few at a time, moving them around
and turning them over. Do not try to put too many in at once.
They should only need to cook for about a minute on each side.
4. Remove from the oil with a large slotted spoon and drain
on some kitchen paper.

Eat immediately with lemon juice and a little finely
chopped parsley.

Insalata di Tonno
Tuna, Eggs, Apples and Mayonnaise

This is an appetizing *antipasto* dish to serve with a selection of salami, cold meats or fish. The recipe comes from a family-run restaurant near Bardi which serves simple country food. One of their specialities is wild boar, and they raise the animals themselves in a field behind the restaurant.

3 EGGS

2 MEDIUM-SIZED APPLES

6 OZ (170 G) TIN OF TUNA IN
   OLIVE OIL

SALT AND FRESHLY GROUND
   BLACK PEPPER

1 TABLESPOON WINE VINEGAR

MAYONNAISE TO COVER

PARSLEY TO GARNISH

1. Boil the eggs until hard; shell and slice thinly.
2. Peel and core the apples, and slice thinly.
3. Empty the tuna fish with its oil into a bowl, and season with the salt and pepper. Add the wine vinegar.
4. Arrange the tuna on the bottom of a small shallow serving-dish. Cover with the thinly sliced eggs and place the sliced apples on top.
5. Put the mayonnaise into a piping bag and pipe it decoratively over the apples. Garnish with a little parsley and serve as soon as possible.

INSALATA DI PATATE CON TONNO
Potato Salad with Tuna

4 MEDIUM–SIZED POTATOES

1 SMALL ONION

SALT AND FRESHLY GROUND BLACK PEPPER

6 OZ (170 G) TIN OF TUNA IN OLIVE OIL

2–3 TABLESPOONS WINE VINEGAR

1 TABLESPOON CHOPPED FRESH PARSLEY

1. Clean the potatoes and boil them in their skins. Allow them to cool and then cut them into slices.
2. Slice the onion very thinly and add to the potatoes. Season with salt and freshly ground black pepper.
3. Put the onion and potatoes into a shallow serving-dish. Add the tuna, either shredded or in small chunks. Just before serving add the wine vinegar and chopped parsley.

INSALATA DI FUNGHI E GAMBERONI
Mushroom and Prawn Salad

½ LB (225 G) FRESH MUSHROOMS
4 OZ (115 G) COOKED PEELED PRAWNS
OLIVE OIL
LEMON JUICE
SALT AND FRESHLY GROUND BLACK PEPPER

1. Wash and drain the mushrooms, and slice them thinly.
2. Rinse the prawns, drain and add to the raw mushrooms in a serving dish.
3. Add enough olive oil to coat the mushrooms and prawns, season with salt and pepper and sprinkle with a little lemon juice.

AUBERGINES AND PRAWNS

To serve 4

1 LARGE AUBERGINE
SALT
8 LARGE UNCOOKED PRAWNS
½ OZ (15 G) BUTTER
1 CLOVE OF GARLIC, CRUSHED
OLIVE OIL
2 TABLESPOONS CHOPPED
   FRESH PARSLEY

4 TABLESPOONS SINGLE OR
   SOURED CREAM
FRESHLY GROUND BLACK
   PEPPER
1 RADICCHIO OR SMALL GREEN
   LETTUCE

1. Dice the aubergine, sprinkle lightly with salt, cover with a heavy plate and leave for 30 minutes.

2. Peel the prawns, cut in half lengthwise and discard the black stringy part. Rinse.

3. In a shallow pan melt the butter and add the crushed garlic and olive oil. When hot add the prawns and most of the parsley (leaving some parsley for decoration). Cook the prawns quickly until pink and then add the aubergines and cook for a further 5 minutes. Add the cream and seasoning and cook for another couple of minutes on a medium heat.

4. Arrange the aubergines and prawns on a bed of crisp lettuce and sprinkle with the remainder of the chopped parsley. Serve immediately.

TOMATOES STUFFED WITH MOZZARELLA AND FRESH BASIL

To serve 4

4 LARGE TOMATOES
3 OZ (85 G) FRESH ITALIAN *MOZZARELLA*
3 TABLESPOONS CHOPPED FRESH BASIL, PLUS ANOTHER
   TEASPOONFUL FOR DECORATION
FRESHLY GROUND BLACK PEPPER

1. Wash the tomatoes and scoop out most of the centre to make room for the stuffing. Stand them on a lightly oiled baking tray.
2. Chop the *mozzarella*, putting aside 4 slices large enough to fit neatly under the top of each tomato, and mix the chopped *mozzarella* with the 3 tablespoons basil and the black pepper.
3. Stuff the tomatoes with this mixture and place a slice of *mozzarella* on each tomato. Sprinkle with a little more basil, put the tomato tops back on, if desired, and bake at Mark 5 (375°F, 190°C) for 20 minutes.

TOMATOES STUFFED WITH SPINACH

To serve 4

4 LARGE TOMATOES
2 OZ (55 G) COOKED FRESH SPINACH
I EGG
3 TABLESPOONS FRESH BREADCRUMBS
½ TEASPOON GRATED NUTMEG
SALT AND PEPPER

1. Wash the tomatoes and remove their centres.
2. In a bowl mix together the cooked spinach, egg, breadcrumbs, nutmeg and seasoning.
3. Fill each tomato with the mixture, place on a buttered tray and bake for 20 minutes at Mark 5 (375°F, 190°C).

TOMATOES STUFFED WITH RICE AND CHEESE

To serve 4

3 OZ (85 G) ARBORIO RICE
4 LARGE TOMATOES
1 OZ (30 G) BUTTER
2 TABLESPOONS FINELY
  CHOPPED ONION

1 TEASPOON CHOPPED FRESH
  BASIL
SALT AND FRESHLY GROUND
  BLACK PEPPER
2 OZ (55 G) FONTINA CHEESE

1. Cook and drain the rice.
2. Wash the tomatoes and scrape out the centres.
3. Melt the butter in a pan and add the onion, basil and seasoning. Cook until the onion is slightly golden.
4. Add the drained rice and cook for another minute.
5. Stuff the tomatoes with the mixture from the pan. Place on an oiled tray, sprinkle with the grated Fontina and bake for 20 minutes at Mark 5 (375°F, 190°C).

POMIDORI CON TONNO
Tomatoes and Tuna

To serve 4

4 LARGE TOMATOES

Tuna mayonnaise

2 OZ (55 G) TUNA FISH
4 OZ (115 G) OLIVE OIL
2 EGG YOLKS
I TEASPOON LEMON JUICE
FRESHLY CHOPPED PARSLEY

1. Wash the tomatoes and cut them in half. Scoop out the middles.
2. Put the tuna through a sieve, with the oil if there is any.
3. Make a mayonnaise (see p. 88) with the oil, egg yolks and lemon juice (if there is oil with the tuna, make sure you don't add too much of it to the mayonnaise). Break the tuna up a little and add it to the mayonnaise.

Stuff the tomatoes with the tuna mayonnaise and sprinkle with a little fresh parsley.

SAUCES

In Italy, sauces have a particularly important role to play as an accompaniment to pasta of various kinds. All these sauces are basically quite simple, though some require long, slow simmering – the aim is to bring out and intensify the natural flavours of the ingredients. As well as the classic meat sauces, Ragù and Sugo di Carne, I have included several recipes for tomato sauce, and an unusual artichoke sauce. And of course there is also a recipe for Pesto, the wonderfully aromatic sauce made from basil. (You will find more sauces for pasta in the next chapter.)

It is a good idea when you are making a sauce for pasta to make double quantities and store half in the fridge or the freezer. Then, if you have to make a meal in a hurry – perhaps when you come in late from work – you only have to cook some pasta and heat up the sauce to go with it to make the main dish; a plate of mixed *antipasto* to start with and a simple salad and fruit to follow could complete the meal.

Sauces are also immensely adaptable. It is worth making *ragù*, for example, in large quantities so that it can be stretched to make several meals: it will make a sauce for pasta, it can be used in a risotto (p. 154), and it is a basic ingredient of lasagne and cannelloni. Tomato sauce is another that has many uses.

As well as sauces to go with pasta, I have given recipes for mayonnaise and salad dressing, and for Salsa Verde, a useful sauce for accompanying cold meats. And there is also a recipe for béchamel, which is required for a number of Italian dishes.

Mayonnaise

The thought of making mayonnaise at home frightens the life out of some people but it really isn't that difficult!

2 EGG YOLKS AT ROOM TEMPERATURE
SALT
½ PINT (275 ML) OLIVE OIL
1 TABLESPOON LEMON JUICE

1. Put the egg yolks into a bowl, which should be large enough to take all the ingredients comfortably. Add a pinch of salt to the yolks and beat well (if possible with an electric whisk) until the yolks are pale yellow in colour and have thickened.
2. Now to add the oil. This is the stage where people often seem to have trouble; the secret is not to rush things at this point but to add the oil drop by drop at first, very slowly, beating all the time. Soon you will see the mixture beginning to emulsify. When about half the oil has been used, add half the lemon juice and continue beating. Now add some more oil – you can work faster now – and the remainder of the lemon juice, but add the last of the lemon juice slowly and keep an eye on the mayonnaise, as you do not want to make it too thin. Finish adding the oil and taste for salt.

Home-made mayonnaise will keep for about three days in the fridge. If you like, you can add other seasonings or fresh herbs to the mayonnaise.

You can also make mayonnaise in a food processor, but again don't be tempted to rush the process.

Olive-oil Dressing

The most important ingredient when making a dressing is the oil. Keep a good-quality cold-pressed olive oil especially for making salad dressing. (There is a wide selection of olive oils on the market. Buy a small quantity initially to test that the strength and flavour are to your liking.)

Italians usually pour the dressing ingredients straight on to the salad after it has been washed and dried. First salt is sprinkled on, then the olive oil is slowly poured on to coat the salad and the vinegar is added drop by drop. This is a basic dressing.

If you prefer, you can mix the dressing separately in a jug, perhaps adding some garlic or fresh herbs, and then pour it on to the salad.

SALSA VERDE
Green Sauce

This sauce is served with cold meats or fish.

3 TABLESPOONS CHOPPED
  PARSLEY
I SMALL CLOVE OF GARLIC,
  CRUSHED
I TABLESPOON CHOPPED
  CAPERS
SALT AND FRESHLY GROUND
  BLACK PEPPER

I TABLESPOON FRESH LEMON
  JUICE OR I TEASPOON WINE
  VINEGAR
6 TABLESPOONS COLD-PRESSED
  OLIVE OIL

Put all the ingredients in a bowl and mix them together
thoroughly.

SALSA BALSAMELLA
Béchamel Sauce

The secret in making béchamel sauce is to add the milk very slowly in order to prevent lumps forming. The milk can be added either hot or cold.

Makes approximately 1 pt (0.6 l) sauce

2 OZ (55 G) BUTTER
4 OZ (115 G) PLAIN FLOUR
1¼ PT (0.7 L) MILK
SALT AND GRATED NUTMEG

1. In a pan large enough to take all the milk, gently melt the butter. Do not let it burn or brown at all.
2. When the butter has melted, remove the pan from the heat and add the flour, stirring continuously with a wooden spoon until you have a smooth paste.
3. Still with the pan off the heat, add about 3 tablespoons of the milk and mix thoroughly. Add another 4–6 tablespoons and stir until the paste has thinned out a little and is completely smooth.
4. Return to the heat and gradually add the rest of the milk. Season and stir until the sauce thickens and coats the back of the wooden spoon.

PESTO

This highly individual, traditional sauce made from fresh basil comes originally from Genoa. It is essential to use a very good quality cold-pressed olive oil as the flavour really does shine through.

The quantities given will make enough for six people; the sauce should lightly coat the pasta only – it should not overwhelm it.

2 GOOD HANDFULS OF
FRESH BASIL LEAVES
I LARGE CLOVE OF GARLIC
I OZ (30 G) PINE KERNELS
1½ OZ (45 G) FRESHLY GRATED
PARMESAN

I OZ (30 G) FRESHLY GRATED
PECORINO
SEA SALT
6–8 TABLESPOONS OLIVE OIL

This is a traditional recipe for making *pesto* in a mortar. It can be made in an electric blender but I find it is never quite as good as when it is made by hand.

1. Put the basil, garlic and pine kernels in a large mortar. Grind and crush thoroughly.
2. Add the two cheeses. Then add the salt and mix together again.
3. Add the olive oil slowly, a little at a time, mixing well.

To store *pesto*, place it in airtight jars and top up with olive oil. It will keep very well like this and it is a much better way of preserving *pesto* than freezing it, although it can be frozen.

TOMATO SAUCES

I find tomato sauces some of the most enjoyable to make, especially when fresh ripe plum tomatoes are available. These give the most wonderful flavour, but if they are not available you can use tinned Italian peeled tomatoes instead.

These sauces really do need to simmer slowly for a long time to allow the sauce to reduce and to develop the full flavour of the ingredients.

Tomato sauce freezes well. Make a large quantity and then divide it into convenient quantities for freezing.

TOMATO SAUCE 1

This is a light, summery sauce, perfect for a hot day. Fresh basil is essential – dried basil cannot be used in this recipe.

2½ LB (1.1 KG) RIPE PLUM TOMATOES
1 OZ (30 G) BUTTER
4 TABLESPOONS COLD-PRESSED OLIVE OIL
1 MEDIUM ONION
4–5 LEAVES OF FRESH BASIL
SALT AND FRESHLY GROUND BLACK PEPPER

1. Wash the tomatoes and cut them into quarters. Place them in a saucepan with approximately ¼ pt (150 ml) cold water. Bring to a brisk boil and simmer for 20 minutes. When cooked put through a sieve or mouli-légumes.
2. In a heavy-bottomed pan melt the butter and add the olive oil. Chop the onion very finely and cook for 2–3 minutes.
3. Add the tomatoes, fresh basil leaves (torn, not chopped) and seasoning. Bring to the boil and simmer gently for 40 minutes.

TOMATO SAUCE 2

When you do not have any fresh basil you can use this recipe for tomato sauce. Although it is so simple, it is extremely good. It must be allowed to cook for long enough to bring out the flavour of the tomatoes.

2½ LB (1.1 KG) RIPE PLUM TOMATOES
1 MEDIUM ONION
2 TABLESPOONS OLIVE OIL
2 TEASPOONS SUGAR
SALT AND FRESHLY GROUND BLACK PEPPER

1. Wash the tomatoes and cut them into quarters. Put into a pan with about ¼ pt (150 ml) cold water. Bring to the boil and simmer for 20 minutes.
2. Add the onion cut in large pieces and bring back to the boil. Add the oil and sugar and simmer for 45 minutes. Season.
3. Discard the onion. Liquidize or pass the sauce through a sieve.

TOMATO SAUCE 3

2½ LB (1.1 KG) RIPE PLUM
  TOMATOES
1 OZ (30 G) BUTTER
3 TABLESPOONS COLD-PRESSED
  OLIVE OIL
1 CLOVE OF GARLIC

1 MEDIUM ONION
2 MEDIUM CARROTS
1 STICK CELERY
SALT AND FRESHLY GROUND
  BLACK PEPPER

1. Wash the tomatoes and cut them into quarters. Put in a pan with ¼ pt (150 ml) cold water. Bring to the boil and simmer for 10 minutes.

2. In a heavy-bottomed pan melt the butter and add the olive oil. Crush the garlic, wash the vegetables and chop them very finely and add to the oil and butter. Cook over medium heat for 5 minutes.

3. Add the tomatoes, liquidized or sieved, bring to the boil and simmer for 40 minutes. Season.

Tomato Sauce with Pancetta

If you cannot find a shop which sells *pancetta*, you would do better to choose one of the other recipes for tomato sauce. Some people use bacon as a substitute for *pancetta*, but it is not really satisfactory.

2 LB (0.9 KG) RIPE PLUM
   TOMATOES
1 OZ (30 G) BUTTER
3 TABLESPOONS OLIVE OIL

1 SMALL ONION
4 OZ *PANCETTA*
SALT AND FRESHLY GROUND
   BLACK PEPPER

1. Wash the tomatoes and cut them into quarters. Put into a pan with $\frac{1}{4}$ pt (150 ml) cold water. Bring to the boil and simmer for 15 minutes.
2. Melt the butter in a heavy-bottomed pan and add the olive oil.
3. Chop the onion very finely and cook for 2 minutes. Chop the *pancetta* and add it to the onion.
4. Sieve the tomatoes, add to the pan, season and simmer gently for 20 minutes.

SUGO DI POMIDORO E FUNGHI SECCHI
Tomato Sauce with Dried Mushrooms

This sauce is made from the wild Italian mushrooms called *porcini*. Although expensive, they are worth every penny – especially when you consider that good-quality meat often costs even more. Ordinary cultivated mushrooms will give an entirely different result.

To serve 4–6 people

1 OZ (30 G) *PORCINI* MUSHROOMS
1 OZ (30 G) BUTTER
3 TABLESPOONS COLD-PRESSED OLIVE OIL
1 MEDIUM ONION
1½ LB (0.7 KG) FRESH PLUM TOMATOES OR A 14 OZ (400 G) TIN ITALIAN PEELED TOMATOES
SALT AND FRESHLY GROUND BLACK PEPPER

1. Soak the mushrooms in a bowl of hot water for 20–30 minutes.
2. In a medium-sized heavy pan melt the butter and add the olive oil. Chop the onion very finely and add to the pan. Cook slowly for 5 minutes. Do not allow the onion to burn or brown.
3. Drain the mushrooms through a sieve lined with absorbent kitchen paper. Retain the water the mushrooms have been soaked in.
4. Chop the mushrooms roughly, add to the pan with the onions and cook for a couple of minutes.
5. Pass the tomatoes through a sieve if tinned, or boil first and then pass through a sieve if fresh, and add to the pan. Season and bring to a brisk boil. Turn down the heat and

simmer gently for 30 minutes, gradually adding the liquid the mushrooms were soaked in. When all the liquid has been added, cook for a further 10 minutes or until the sauce has reduced sufficiently.

This sauce can accompany virtually any kind of pasta and can also be used for risotto.

SALSA DI TOPINAMBUR
Jerusalem Artichoke Sauce

This is an unusual sauce for pasta, and it is very easy to prepare. Don't be tempted to eat too much of it, though, as it can be rather indigestible – and, as with all pasta sauces, it should lightly coat the pasta, not hide it.

I LB (450 G) JERUSALEM
   ARTICHOKES
I OZ (30 G) BUTTER
2 TABLESPOONS OLIVE OIL
I TABLESPOON CHOPPED
   PARSLEY

I CLOVE OF GARLIC
SALT AND FRESHLY GROUND
   BLACK PEPPER
I TABLESPOON SINGLE OR
   SOURED CREAM

1. Peel the artichokes and cook in boiling salted water for 20–25 minutes.
2. Purée the artichokes in a liquidizer or pass them through a sieve.
3. Melt the butter in a shallow pan, and add the oil, parsley and crushed garlic clove. Wait until the butter sizzles and then add the artichokes and seasoning and cook for a few minutes. Just before serving add the cream.

RAGÙ

Ragù is a sauce made from meat and tomatoes simmered together for a long time. The sauce came originally from Bologna, but it varies considerably from one part of Italy to another, and even from one cook to another. This is my mother-in-law's recipe – she makes the best *ragù* I have tasted. You can use lean beef instead of veal if you prefer.

I MEDIUM ONION	2 LB (0.9 KG) RIPE TOMATOES OR
I CARROT	A 22 OZ (629 G) TIN OF
I OZ (30 G) BUTTER	ITALIAN PEELED TOMATOES
4 TABLESPOONS OLIVE OIL	2–3 LADLEFULS CHICKEN OR
I LB STEWING OR LEAN PIE	VEAL STOCK
VEAL	SALT AND FRESHLY GROUND
A SPRIG OF FRESH ROSEMARY	BLACK PEPPER

Roughly chop the onion and carrot. Melt the butter and 2 tablespoons of the oil in a large, heavy pan. Add the onion, carrot, meat and rosemary. Cook briskly until the meat is lightly browned.

2. Remove the meat and vegetables (leaving the juices in the pan) and chop in the food processor – or turn on to a large wooden board and chop by hand using a mezzaluna. The meat should be chopped a little more coarsely than minced meat.

3. Return the meat and vegetables to the pan and add the tinned tomatoes, sieved, or, if you are using fresh tomatoes, simmer them in about 1 in (2.5 cm) of water until soft and then sieve them into the meat. Add one ladleful of stock.

4. Season the sauce, add the remainder of the oil and bring to a brisk boil. Boil for 10 minutes and then simmer for at least 1½ hours, adding a little more stock if necessary.

Just before serving 3 tablespoons of single cream or milk can be added to make the sauce smooth.

When making this sauce it is a good idea to make a larger quantity than you need as it freezes very well and is used in many pasta dishes.

SUGO DI CARNE
Meat Sauce

I MEDIUM ONION
I CARROT
A STICK OF CELERY
I LB (450 G) LEAN BEEF
I OZ (30 G) BUTTER
3 TABLESPOONS OLIVE OIL
I TABLESPOON FINELY
  CHOPPED PARSLEY

2 BAY LEAVES
SALT AND FRESHLY GROUND
  BLACK PEPPER
½ PINT (275 ML) STOCK
I TEASPOON TOMATO PURÉE

1. Wash and dice the vegetables and chop the meat.
2. Heat the butter and olive oil, and add the onion, parsley, bay leaves and meat. Season and cook for about 10 minutes on a medium heat. Add the carrot and celery and cook for another couple of minutes. Remove the bay leaves.
3. Place all the ingredients, including the contents of the pan, in a food processor and chop, but not too finely. The meat should be as fine as minced beef. If you don't have a food processor, use a mezzaluna for this.
4. Return everything to the pan, and add the stock and tomato purée. Bring to a brisk boil and cook for 3 minutes; then turn down the heat and simmer for 1 hour.

I PRIMI PIATTI
THE FIRST COURSE

In England we have adopted pasta dishes and turned them into a meal in themselves, but in Italy it is usual to have a dish of pasta, *gnocchi* or risotto before the main course of the meal. As there will be meat or fish to follow, the sauce should just flavour the pasta, but should not dominate it.

The names given to the various pasta shapes are extremely confusing, as different regions have different names for the same type of pasta and, to make matters worse, the same word may mean different kinds of pasta in different regions.

In many dishes you can use whatever type of pasta you happen to have available, but some shapes – for example *fusilli* – are particularly good for picking up a creamy sauce; others – such as cannelloni and lasagne – are used for dishes which are baked in the oven.

I have given instructions for making your own fresh pasta, which is not difficult, but it does take time, especially if you do not have a pasta machine. However, fresh pasta is now widely available in the shops in Britain. In the early days of Fratelli Camisa, pasta was made by hand in the shop, and took hours of hard work. Today the pasta is made in quantity by machine, but it is still superior to dry pasta. Remember that fresh pasta will cook much more quickly than dry, so be careful not to overcook it.

I have included several pasta dishes in this chapter and you will find more sauces that can be used with pasta in the previous chapter.

Despite its great popularity, pasta is not the only first-course dish – risotto and *gnocchi* are also popular and, like pasta, they can be served with a variety of different sauces.

Depending on appetite, some of the recipes in this chapter – Risotto con Ragù and Spaghetti alla Gorgonzola are examples – are equally suitable as main-course lunch or supper dishes, followed by a salad.

PASTA FATTA IN CASA
Home-made Pasta

Making pasta yourself requires patience and a little hard work, but once you have made it a few times it will become second nature. If you have a pasta-making machine (see p. 15), it will do the work of rolling out the pasta for you – the most difficult part of the process to master – but you will still have to mix the dough by hand.

To make pasta at home you will need the following:

1. a large wooden board or work-top; don't try to make pasta on a surface which is too small;

2. a long rolling-pin – ideally about 20–24 in (50–60 cm) – or a pasta-making machine;

3. a clean surface where you can lay out the pasta once it is made;

4. a broad-bladed knife for cutting the pasta.

Obviously you will need to measure the quantities of flour and water to start with, but as you become more used to making pasta, you will find that you get to know the quantities required; the exact amount of flour will in any case depend on the size of the eggs and the absorbency of the flour you are using.

To serve 6

1 LB (450 G) PLAIN FLOUR
3 OR 4 EGGS (DEPENDING ON SIZE)
A FEW DROPS OF OLIVE OIL
SALT (THIS IS OPTIONAL, AS THE PASTA WILL BE COOKED IN
    SALTED WATER)
FLOUR FOR DUSTING THE BOARD OR WORK SURFACE

First see that the work surface is completely cleared; make sure that you have enough room to work in and have all the ingredients to hand.

1. Pour the flour on to the board or work surface in a mound – or use a bowl – and make a well in the middle.
2. Next, break the eggs straight into the well, and mix with your fingers – if you feel that this is going to be a little difficult or messy, break the eggs into a cup, beat lightly and then pour into the well. Add a few drops of olive oil and 1 tablespoon of water to the eggs in the well (or in the cup if you have used one).
3. Now begin to fold in the flour from around the sides of the mound and mix it in with the eggs. You have to do this reasonably quickly or you will find that the eggs begin to trickle down the work surface. Use one hand to support the flour if you can. The ingredients will soon begin to bind together and make a ball of dough.
4. Once you have a ball of dough you can begin kneading. Wash and dry your hands, sprinkle a little flour on the work surface and then, with the heel of your palm, press and push the dough away from you. Knead and turn the dough; if it is sticky, add a little flour. The kneading will take about 10 minutes and at the end of this time the dough should be smooth and elastic. (See diagram.)

If you have a pasta-making machine, you can now use it to complete the process, following the instructions that come with the machine. Otherwise, continue with steps 5–10.

5. Place the dough in a bowl, cover it with cling film and leave it to rest for at least 15 minutes.

6. Cut the dough in half, and put one half back in the bowl. Cover it again to prevent it from drying out.

7. Flour the rolling-pin and the work surface. Place the dough on the work surface and gently roll it out, rotating it from time to time as you do so, so that you have an even round shape. Be careful not to press too hard or the dough will stick to the work surface, and always roll away from yourself. Continue until the sheet of dough is about $\frac{1}{8}$ in (3 mm) thick.

8. The next stage is the most difficult. The aim is to *stretch* the sheet of dough, using your hands and the rolling-pin; the pin is *not* used to flatten the dough, as it is when making pastry. You should end up with a sheet of dough so thin that it is almost transparent.

Wrap the far end of the circle of dough round the rolling-pin, and roll the pin back and forth without pressing down on it; at the same time, use the heels of your hands to pull and stretch the dough out from the centre of the pin towards the ends. You will have to repeat this rolling and stretching process quite a few times, until the pasta is as thin as you want it, and you will have to work fairly quickly, as after 10 minutes or so the pasta will no longer be pliable, and will crack when you try to stretch it.

9. When you have made the sheet of pasta thin enough, it should be left to dry out for a while – let it hang over the side of the table covered with a clean cloth, turning it after about 10 minutes. (If the kitchen is cold or damp it may take longer.) While it is drying you can roll out the second piece of dough.

10. When the pasta is dry enough you can cut it into the shape of pasta you require. (If you are making stuffed pasta you must use the dough as soon as it is made, without leaving it to dry out.) *Tagliatelle*, narrow strips of flat pasta, is one of the easiest shapes to make.

To make *tagliatelle*, roll up the sheet of pasta like a newspaper, making a flat roll about ¾ in (2 cm) wide. Steady the roll with one hand and cut the pasta roll across into small strips – for *tagliatelle* they should be about ¼ in (6 mm) wide. Open out the *tagliatelle*, place on a clean cloth and leave it for about 10 minutes. If you don't want to use it all immediately, you can keep any that is left over in the freezer.

Now, that wasn't too bad, was it!

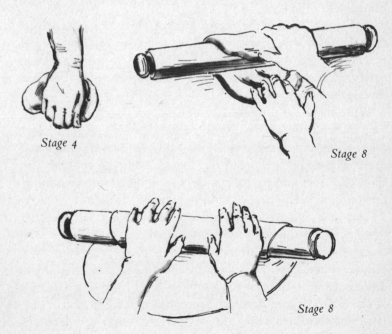

Stage 4

Stage 8

Stage 8

PASTA VERDE
Green Pasta with Spinach

To make *pasta verde* spinach is added to the pasta dough. As well as making the pasta green it also makes it slightly creamier and gives it a heavier consistency.

Pasta verde is made in the same way as ordinary pasta. For every 7–8 oz (200–225 g), you need to add 6 oz (170 g) fresh spinach, cooked, drained and squeezed between two plates. The spinach is chopped very finely, added with the whole eggs into the well in the flour and mixed together with the fingers or a fork, and then the flour is gradually drawn in from around the sides of the well.

COOKING PASTA

Pasta is one of the simplest foods to cook, so why people get into such a mess I don't know! However, I think one of the problems may be using too small a pan and too little water. You need 6–7 pt (3.4–4 l) water for every 1 lb (450 g) pasta, so use a pan large enough to hold both the water and the pasta. When the water has boiled and not before, add salt according to taste (1–1½ tablespoons). Next add the pasta, all at the same time, not bit by bit. Dried spaghetti and other long pasta has to be held until it has softened in the hot water and can be bent round to fit the pan. When the pasta is in the pan, give it a stir to prevent it from sticking. Once the water has come to the boil again, you can cover the pot if you like, although many Italians don't bother. Cook until the pasta is *al dente*; *al dente* means firm to the bite, very slightly resistant – it must not be soggy. Add some cold water and then turn the pasta out into a colander. Shake the colander to get rid of any excess water and serve immediately. Never leave pasta to keep warm.

When cooking fresh pasta remember this literally only takes 2 minutes. Do not overcook fresh pasta, especially if you have taken the trouble to make it yourself – you will ruin it. Put the cooked pasta into a warmed serving-dish, add the sauce and mix them together well. The pasta should be coated with the sauce, but should not be overwhelmed by it.

So there we are – what could be more simple!

DIFFERENT TYPES OF PASTA

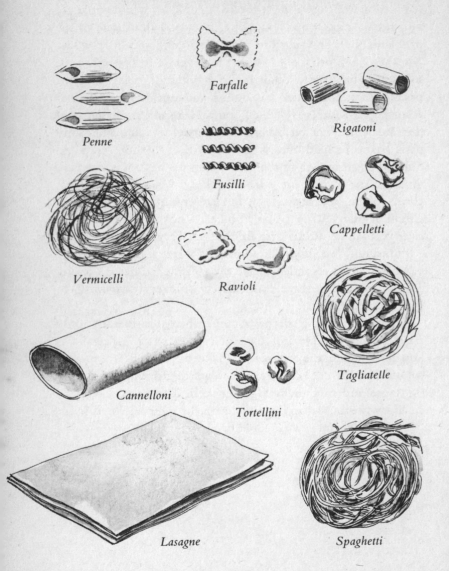

Farfalle

Penne

Rigatoni

Fusilli

Vermicelli

Cappelletti

Ravioli

Cannelloni

Tagliatelle

Tortellini

Lasagne

Spaghetti

SPAGHETTI CON OLIO E AGLIO
Spaghetti with Olive Oil and Garlic

This recipe is delicious, extremely simple and also very cheap.

To serve 4

8 TABLESPOONS OLIVE OIL
1–2 CLOVES OF GARLIC
SALT
1 TABLESPOON FINELY
  CHOPPED FRESH PARSLEY

1 LB (450 G) SPAGHETTI
FRESHLY GROUND BLACK
  PEPPER

1. Bring the water for the pasta to the boil, and put in the spaghetti.
2. While the spaghetti is cooking, heat the olive oil in a small pan with the crushed or finely chopped garlic (depending on how much garlic you like), a little salt and parsley. Cook gently for about 3 minutes.
3. When the pasta is ready, drain it and place in a warmed serving dish. Pour over the garlic and olive oil, mix well together; add as much pepper as you like and mix again.

Serve immediately.

LUMACHE ALLA TARSOGNO
Lumache *with Walnut and Cream Sauce*

This is a recipe from Tarsogno, near Parma, the village where my husband's family comes from.

3 OZ (85 G) SHELLED
  WALNUTS
1 OZ (30 G) FRESH BASIL
7 FL OZ (200 ML) FRESH
  SINGLE CREAM
SALT AND FRESHLY GROUND
  BLACK PEPPER

1 OZ (30 G) UNSALTED BUTTER
4 OZ (115 G) *PANCETTA*
  (TWO SLICES)
1 LB (450 G) *LUMACHE*
  (PASTA SHELLS)
2 OZ (55 G) FRESHLY GRATED
  PARMESAN

1. Finely chop the walnuts and basil and mix with the cream; season to taste with salt and pepper.
2. Heat the butter in a large frying-pan over a low heat, taking care not to let it burn. Chop the *pancetta* into small cubes and add to the butter in pan, stirring it so that it browns slowly.
3. Cook the pasta in a large saucepan with plenty of water for 2–3 minutes for fresh pasta, about 10–15 for dried. Drain the pasta and add it to the ham in the frying-pan. Now quickly add the cream sauce, stirring all the time.

Serve with a sprinkling of grated parmesan cheese.

FARFALLE ALL'ALPINA
Farfalle *with Spinach and* Ricotta

The combination of spinach and *ricotta* cheese is frequently used as a filling for cannelloni and other stuffed pasta, but here it makes a sauce for plain pasta. Like many pasta dishes, this is very quickly prepared and cooked.

Serves 4–6

8 OZ (225 G) FRESH SPINACH
BUTTER
SALT
10 OZ (285 G) *RICOTTA*
  CHEESE
1 SMALL CARTON NATURAL
  YOGHURT

6 OZ (170 G) FRESHLY GRATED
  PARMESAN
PINCH OF FRESHLY GRATED
  NUTMEG
1 LB (450 G) *FARFALLE*
  (PASTA BOWS)

1. Wash the spinach thoroughly at least three times, shred into strips and cook for about a minute in a small pan with a little butter and a pinch of salt.
2. Put the *ricotta* into a medium-size mixing bowl and slowly stir in the yoghurt, 2 oz (55 g) parmesan cheese and a pinch of nutmeg. Warm this mixture carefully in a double saucepan, or place the mixing bowl over a saucepan of simmering water. Add the spinach and cook gently for a few minutes, watching to check that the mixture does not boil.
3. Cook the *farfalle* in a saucepan for the required amount of time. Drain the pasta and pour the sauce over. Mix together and serve with plenty of parmesan cheese.

SPAGHETTI ALLA GORGONZOLA
Spaghetti with Gorgonzola

To serve 5

This is a very tasty dish and very quick to prepare, but it is quite rich, so serve small portions. Or serve it as a lunch dish, followed by salad.

4 OZ (115 G) GORGONZOLA CHEESE	1 SMALL STICK OF CELERY, CHOPPED
4 OZ (115 G) FRESH *RICOTTA* CHEESE	SALT AND FRESHLY GROUND BLACK PEPPER
½ CLOVE CRUSHED GARLIC	1 LB (450 G) FRESH SPAGHETTI
2 TABLESPOONS SINGLE CREAM	1 OZ (30 G) UNSALTED BUTTER

1. Place all the ingredients except the spaghetti and butter in a blender and blend until soft and creamy. (If you don't have a blender, pound them in a bowl with a wooden spoon.) If the sauce is a little thick add a few drops of milk.

2. Cook the spaghetti, drain and place in a warmed serving dish. Pour over the sauce and butter and mix well.

VERMICELLI AL TONNO
Vermicelli *and* Tuna

I SMALL ONION
I OZ (30 G) UNSALTED BUTTER
4 TABLESPOONS OLIVE OIL
6 OZ TIN (170 G) ITALIAN
   TUNA
3–4 CAPERS

I STICK CELERY
2 OZ (55 G) STONED SMALL
   BLACK OLIVES, HALVED
SALT AND PEPPER
I LB (450 G) FRESH TOMATOES
   (RIPE)
I LB (450 G) *VERMICELLI*

1. Chop the onion finely and add to the melted butter and oil in a large shallow pan. Cook until the onion is slightly golden.

2. Shred the tuna and add to the onion with the capers, chopped celery and olives. Cool for about 2 minutes and then season with salt and pepper (be careful with the salt though, as the tuna and olives may be salty). Add the tomatoes, chopped, bring everything to a brisk boil and simmer for 15 minutes.

3. In the meantime, cook and drain the *vermicelli*, making sure that it is not overcooked – it cooks very quickly.

4. Put the *vermicelli* into a warmed serving-dish, add the tuna sauce, mix together and serve immediately.

TAGLIATELLE CON PEPERONI E GAMBARETTI
Tagliatelle *with Peppers and Prawns*

This is a very attractive and colourful dish and makes a good main-course lunch or supper dish. It can be served with a simple salad and a good bottle of chilled white wine.

6 LARGE UNCOOKED PRAWNS
I SMALL YELLOW PEPPER
I SMALL RED PEPPER
OLIVE OIL
I CLOVE OF GARLIC, CRUSHED
I TABLESPOON FRESHLY
  CHOPPED PARSLEY

SALT AND FRESHLY GROUND
  BLACK PEPPER
½ PINT (275 ML) BASIC TOMATO
  SAUCE (see p. 93)
I LB (450 G) FRESH SPINACH
  TAGLIATELLE

1. Put on the water for the pasta.
2. Peel and wash the prawns – cut down the back of each prawn and remove the black vein
3. Clean the peppers and cut into thin strips.
4. Heat the oil in a shallow pan, add the garlic, parsley and peppers and cook for 2 minutes. Then add the prawns and cook until they go slightly pink. Season.
5. Add the tomato sauce, bring to the boil and simmer for 15 minutes.
6. Cook and drain the pasta, put into a serving-dish, add the sauce and serve immediately.

RIGATONI ALLA CREMA
Rigatoni *and Cheese Sauce*

To serve 4

I LB (450 G) *RIGATONI*
½ PT (275 ML) BÉCHAMEL
   SAUCE (see p. 91)
2 OZ (55 G) FRESHLY GRATED
   PARMESAN
SEASONING

¼ TEASPOON FRESHLY GRATED
   NUTMEG
FRESHLY GROUND BLACK
   PEPPER
2 TABLESPOONS BREADCRUMBS

1. Boil the water for the pasta in a large saucepan.
2. Prepare the béchamel sauce, adding the seasoning and nutmeg.
3. Cool and drain the pasta and put it into a shallow oven-proof dish. Pour the béchamel sauce over the pasta, mixing well, sprinkle with the cheese and breadcrumbs and put under a hot grill until the top is golden brown and crispy.

PAGLIA E FIENO
Fettucine *with Cream and Peas*

Paglia e fieno ('straw and hay') makes an appetizing dish for a dinner party, with the green and yellow *fettucine* and the creamy sauce. (*Fettucine* are slightly narrower than *tagliatelle* and thicker.

To serve 4

2 OZ (55 G) BUTTER
I TABLESPOON OLIVE OIL
I TABLESPOON FINELY
  CHOPPED SHALLOT
6 FL OZ (170 ML) SINGLE
  CREAM
4 TABLESPOONS SMALL PEAS
  (FRESH IF POSSIBLE)

2 OZ (55 G) GRATED
  PARMESAN
8 OZ (225 G) YELLOW
  NOODLES
8 OZ (225 G) GREEN NOODLES
SALT AND FRESHLY GROUND
  BLACK PEPPER

1. Put the water on for the pasta.
2. In a shallow heavy-bottomed pan melt the butter, add the olive oil, and sauté the chopped shallot until lightly golden. Add the cream and cook gently over a low heat until cream starts to thicken.
3. Add the peas and half the grated parmesan. Leave on a very low heat.
4. When the water for the pasta is boiling, put in first the yellow pasta and then the green – the green will cook in a shorter time.
5. Drain the pasta, transfer it to a warmed dish, season, add the sauce and the remaining grated parmesan and serve immediately.

SPAGHETTI ALLA CARBONARA
Spaghetti with Eggs and Pancetta

This dish is of Roman origin, and is popular all over Italy.

To serve 4

1 LB (450 G) SPAGHETTI
4 OZ (115 G) *PANCETTA*
1 TABLESPOON OLIVE OIL
3 EGG YOLKS
2 TABLESPOONS SINGLE CREAM
SALT AND FRESHLY GROUND
 BLACK PEPPER
2 OZ (55 G) FRESHLY GRATED
 PARMESAN

1. Put on the water for the spaghetti, as the sauce only takes a few minutes to make.
2. While the spaghetti is cooking, cut the *pancetta* up into smallish pieces and add to a large heavy frying-pan with the olive oil. Cook for a few minutes and then drain off most of the fat, leaving just a trace in the pan. Remove the pan from the heat.
3. Beat the egg yolks in a bowl and then add the cream, seasoning and half the cheese.
4. The spaghetti should be cooked by now; place the pan with the *pancetta* in it on a very low heat (as low as possible), add the drained spaghetti and stir.
5. Add the egg mixture, stirring all the time. The eggs will cook instantly in the hot pasta.

Serve immediately with the rest of the parmesan.

FUSILLI VERDI CON SALSA GORGONZOLA
Fusilli Verdi *with Gorgonzola Sauce*

This sauce is extremely rich, so it is best served in modest quantities as a first course rather than as a main course. It should be followed by a plain dish. (The amount of pasta given here is intended for a first course.)

To serve 4

6 OZ (170 G) GORGONZOLA
4 TABLESPOONS SINGLE CREAM
FRESHLY GROUND BLACK
   PEPPER

10–12 OZ (280–340 G)
   FUSILLI VERDI (FRESH IF
   POSSIBLE)
FRESHLY GRATED PARMESAN

1. Start to cook the pasta straight away as the sauce only takes a few minutes to make.
2. In a small pan break up the Gorgonzola with a wooden spoon and melt it slowly with the cream. Season with the pepper and allow the cheese and cream to simmer for a few minutes. If the sauce becomes a little thick you can add a teaspoon or two of milk.
3. Drain the pasta and put it into a warmed serving dish. Add the sauce. Mix together with a little grated parmesan and serve immediately.

This sauce is also delicious with *polenta*.

MANFREDINE ALLA PARMIGIANA
Pasta with Sausage and Aubergine

The secret of this recipe is good Italian pork sausages, spicy or mild depending on which you prefer. If the sausages are very spicy adjust the seasoning accordingly.

To serve 4

I MEDIUM-SIZED AUBERGINE
SALT
12 OZ (340 G) FRESH ITALIAN
    PORK SAUSAGES
FRESH THYME
1 MEDIUM-SIZED ONION
1 GARLIC CLOVE
6 TABLESPOONS OLIVE OIL
12 OZ (340 G) FRESH
    TOMATOES

½ WINE-GLASS DRY WHITE
    WINE (WATER WILL DO
    INSTEAD)
SALT AND FRESHLY GROUND
    BLACK PEPPER
I LB (450 G) *MANFREDINE*
    OR OTHER PASTA
A KNOB OF BUTTER

1. Peel the aubergine and cut into small pieces. Sprinkle with a little salt, cover and leave for ½ hour with a heavy weight on top. Dab with kitchen paper to squeeze out moisture.
2. Skin the sausages and mix the fresh thyme with the meat. Refrigerate until needed.
3. Finely chop the onion and crush the garlic. In a large frying-pan warm the oil, add the onion and garlic and cook on a medium heat for 2 minutes until the onion is lightly golden.
4. Add the sausage meat and cook on a medium heat for about 5 minutes.
5. Add the sieved tomatoes and wine or water, season and bring to a brisk boil. Turn down the heat and simmer for 20 minutes.

6. While the sauce is simmering cook the pasta. Drain and put into a rectangular warmed serving-dish with a knob of butter. Add the pasta and sauce, mix well and serve.

Spaghetti alle Vongole
Spaghetti with Clams

Good quality tinned clams can be used for this sauce, but they are very expensive.

To serve 4

3 DOZEN CLAMS	1 LB (450 G) SKINNED
3 TABLESPOONS OIL	TOMATOES
2 SHALLOTS	SALT AND PEPPER
PARSLEY	1 LB (450 G) SPAGHETTI
1 CLOVE OF GARLIC	

1. Clams often contain sand. To remove it, submerge the clams in cold water for about 20 minutes or so. Drain off the water and scrub the clams thoroughly in clean water. Repeat until the water runs clear.
2. Put the clams into a pan over a strong heat, shaking the pan all the time until they open. Strain the clams and remove their shells.
3. Start to cook the spaghetti.
4. In a heavy-bottomed pan heat the oil and add the shallots, parsley and garlic, all finely chopped. Cook for 2 minutes.
5. Add the clams and cook for a further 30 seconds.
6. Now add the fresh sieved tomatoes and bring to a slow boil. Season with salt and pepper, and simmer for 10 minutes.
7. Drain the pasta and transfer it to a warmed serving-dish. Pour the clam sauce over the spaghetti and serve immediately.

N.B. Cheese is never served with this dish.

PENNE WITH CLAM, TOMATO AND LEEK SAUCE

See p. 127 for details of how to prepare clams.

1½ LB (0.7 KG) FRESH TOMATOES
1 OZ (30 G) BUTTER
2 TABLESPOONS OLIVE OIL
1 GARLIC CLOVE, CRUSHED
PARSLEY

1 SHALLOT, FINELY CHOPPED
1 CARROT, CHOPPED
1 LEEK, CHOPPED
3 DOZEN CLAMS
1 LB (450 G) *PENNE*
SALT AND PEPPER

1. Cut the tomatoes into quarters, put them into a large saucepan, cover with water and bring to the boil. Simmer for about 15 minutes.
2. When the tomatoes are cooked, put them through a sieve and leave to one side.
3. Put on the water for the pasta (about 6–7 pt, 3.4–4 l).
4. In a heavy-bottomed pan or a frying-pan, melt the butter with the olive oil and garlic. Add half of the parsley, the shallot, carrot and leek and cook for 2 minutes; then add the shelled clams.
5. When the clams have cooked for about 1 minute add the sieved tomatoes, bring to the boil, add the rest of the parsley and then simmer for about 10–15 minutes. Check for salt; it should not really need any as the clams are quite salty.
6. Meanwhile, cook the pasta, drain it and put it into a warmed serving dish.
7. Pour the sauce over the pasta and mix thoroughly. Serve immediately.

PASTA SHELLS WITH MUSSELS

I LB (450 G) RIPE TOMATOES
2 TABLESPOONS OLIVE OIL
I CLOVE OF GARLIC, CRUSHED
I TABLESPOON FINELY
  CHOPPED PARSLEY
8–10 MUSSELS PER PERSON
  (PREPARED AS DESCRIBED
ON P. 73 AND THEN TAKEN
  FROM THEIR SHELLS)
SALT AND FRESHLY GROUND
  BLACK PEPPER
I LB (450 G) PASTA SHELLS

1. Put on the water for the pasta.
2. Roughly chop the tomatoes. Boil them for a few minutes and then pass them through a sieve.
3. In a shallow pan heat the oil, add the garlic, parsley and mussels and cook for a minute or so. Add the tomatoes, salt and pepper and cook gently for 10 minutes.
4. Meanwhile, cook the pasta and place it in a warmed serving-dish.
5. Pour the sauce over the pasta.

PENNE ALLA CASALINGA
Penne *with Olive Oil and Tomato and Basil Sauce*

The secret of this recipe is to use really fresh ingredients. Try to obtain ripe plum tomatoes and fresh basil; dried basil does not give the same result or flavour. Because the recipe is so simple, the use of a good cold-pressed olive oil will really be noticed here and will give it a wonderful flavour.

To serve 4

6 TABLESPOONS COLD-PRESSED
   OLIVE OIL
I GARLIC CLOVE
ABOUT 6 BASIL LEAVES, TORN
   INTO PIECES
1½ LB (680 G) FRESH PLUM
   TOMATOES

SALT AND PEPPER
I LB (450 G) *PENNE*
3 OZ (85 G) FRESHLY GRATED
   PARMESAN

1. In a heavy-bottomed, medium-sized pan, warm the olive oil, add the crushed garlic and the fresh basil, and cook for 2 minutes.
2. Prepare the fresh tomatoes by boiling them for 10 minutes and then putting them through a sieve. Add the sieved tomatoes to the oil, garlic and basil, which should be really hot – let the tomatoes sizzle as they go in. Bring to a slow boil and then immediately turn down the heat to a low simmer for 15 minutes. Season and simmer for another 10 minutes.

Cook the *penne*, drain, transfer to a warmed serving-dish and mix in the tomato sauce. Serve the parmesan separately.

This sauce freezes well.

CANNELLONI WITH SPINACH AND RICOTTA

The list of ingredients required for this recipe makes the preparation look like a whole week's work, but you will find that it is not so bad as it seems. You can use either tomato sauce or *ragù*, whichever you prefer, and you can buy fresh pasta or make your own. (But do not use dried pasta – it will not taste as good.)

One of the secrets of making successful cannelloni, I think, is not trying to stuff them too full. Also, I prefer cannelloni made with a sauce which is not too heavy.

To serve 6

The pasta

A SHEET OF HOME–MADE PASTA
   MADE FROM:
8 OZ (225 G) PLAIN FLOUR

2 LARGE EGGS
I TEASPOON SALT

I RECIPE TOMATO SAUCE
   (P. 93) OR *RAGÙ* (P. 101)

The stuffing

1½ LB (680 G) FRESH SPINACH
2 EGGS
2–3 OZ (55–85 G) FRESH
   BREADCRUMBS

I TABLESPOON OLIVE OIL
SALT AND FRESHLY GROUND
   BLACK PEPPER
3 OZ (85 G) *RICOTTA*

I RECIPE BECHAMEL SAUCE
   (P. 91)
FRESHLY GRATED PARMESAN

1. If you are making the pasta yourself, follow the instructions on p. 108. Cut the pasta into 3 × 4 in (8 × 10 cm) rectangles. For this recipe you will need twelve strips; two for each person should be ample.

2. Prepare the tomato or meat sauce.

3. Wash the spinach thoroughly at least three times. Discard any hard stalks. When clean, put into a large saucepan with a lid on over a medium heat and cook without water for about 3–5 minutes. Hold the pan in one hand over the heat and the lid in the other hand and shake the pan until the spinach has reduced.

4. Drain the spinach and press it between two plates to squeeze out all the water – it is essential that all the water is removed. Chop finely either in a food processor or with a mezzaluna. Add the remainder of the ingredients for the stuffing and mix well. Refrigerate for ½ hour.

5. Make the béchamel sauce.

6. In a large pan bring 6–7 pt (3.4–4 l) water to the boil – when it is boiling, add the salt and carefully drop in the pasta strips. After the water has returned to the boil let it continue to cook for about a minute. Cook the pasta in batches of 4 at a time, gently moving them around the pan with a wooden spoon to prevent them from sticking. When it is ready lift out the pasta with a slotted spoon, dip into a bowl of cold water and then place on a clean cloth on the work surface. Repeat until all the pasta is ready.

7. Set the oven to Mark 6 (400°F, 200°C).

8. At this point make sure that you have enough room and a clean working surface. Have the bowl of stuffing ready at your side. In the bottom of a rectangular oven dish spread a couple of tablespoons of each of the sauces evenly, for the cannelloni to sit on. Take a strip of the pasta and place a heaped tablespoon of stuffing on it, leaving about ½ in (12 mm) empty all round the edge. Then roll up the pasta and

place it in the dish with the join underneath. Repeat with all the rectangles of pasta, leaving a little space between each in the dish.

9. Pour over the tomato sauce or *ragù* and then pour over the béchamel but do not cover it all over with béchamel – the *ragù* or tomato sauce should show through. Sprinkle with freshly grated parmesan and bake in the middle of the oven for about 20 minutes until the top is lightly golden and there is a slight crust round the edges.

LASAGNE VERDI AL FORNO

Everyone is familiar with lasagne – as served in restaurants, or as a ready-made meal in a plastic pack which only has to be reheated – but in England the word *lasagne* covers a multitude of variants, many of which are only loosely connected with the Italian original. The lasagne that you make yourself, with home-made pasta and fresh béchamel, is something quite different. It does take a long time to prepare, but it is well worth the effort. If you don't have time to make your own pasta you can buy fresh pasta instead. Dried lasagne is a poor substitute.

To serve 6

The pasta

1 LB (450 G) FRESH SPINACH
1 LB (450 G) STRONG PLAIN
   FLOUR
3 EGGS
SALT

1 RECIPE SUGO DI CARNE
   (P. 103) OR RAGÚ
1 RECIPE BÉCHAMEL SAUCE
   (P. 91)
SALT
3 OZ (85 G) FRESHLY GRATED
   PARMESAN

1. Wash the spinach thoroughly, removing the stalks. Leave the spinach leaves dripping with water and put into a large pan; cook, shaking the pan from time to time, for about 5 minutes.
2. To make the pasta for lasagne, follow the recipe for home-made pasta (p. 108), adding the spinach, chopped very finely, with the eggs.
3. Cut the pasta into rectangular pieces about 3 × 4 in (8 × 10 cm).

4. Prepare the meat and béchamel sauces.

5. Prepare a bowl of cold water and a clean surface on which to lay out the cooked lasagne. Boil the water for the pasta – about 7–8 pt (4–4.5 l) – add the salt and drop in the pasta, about 4–6 pieces at a time. Stir and cook for about a minute. Remove the pasta from the water with a slotted spoon, dip into the cold water and lay out flat. Continue until all the pasta is cooked; when it is all done, pat dry.

6. Set the oven to Mark 6 (400°F, 200°C).

7. Put a little of the meat sauce in the bottom of a rectangular ovenproof dish, at least 3 in (7.5 cm) deep and 12 in (30 cm) long. Add pieces of pasta over the sauce to cover the bottom of the dish. Try not to let the pasta curl up the sides of the dish, as it will become burnt and dry.

8. Spread a little meat sauce over the pasta, just to cover it. Then add a layer of béchamel sauce and a sprinkling of parmesan. Continue with layers of pasta, meat sauce, béchamel and parmesan until all the pasta has been used.

9. Finish with a layer of meat sauce and a layer of béchamel. The final layer of béchamel sauce should be quite thick but should not completely cover the lasagne. Sprinkle with the remainder of the parmesan and cook in the oven for 25–30 minutes or until slightly golden on top.

You can use ordinary home-made pasta (p. 108) for making lasagne if you prefer, instead of *lasagne verdi* made from spinach.

RAVIOLI

Ravioli are square parcels of pasta filled with a savoury stuffing. Ravioli with the stuffing given here is best served with a tomato sauce or simply with butter and freshly grated parmesan.

For the pasta

1 LB (450 G) STRONG WHITE PLAIN FLOUR
SALT
3 EGGS
4–6 TABLESPOONS WARM MILK

For the stuffing

1 OZ (30 G) BUTTER
2 SHALLOTS
8 OZ (225 G) STEWING OR PIE VEAL
3 TABLESPOONS FRESH BREADCRUMBS
2 EGGS, BEATEN
2 TABLESPOONS OLIVE OIL
2 OZ (55 G) FRESHLY GRATED PARMESAN

SALT AND FRESHLY GROUND BLACK PEPPER
$\frac{1}{2}$ TEASPOON GRATED NUTMEG
4 TABLESPOONS WARM MILK
1 OZ (30 G) *PROSCIUTTO CRUDO*
1 TABLESPOON CHOPPED PARSLEY

To make the stuffing

1. Melt the butter in a shallow pan and sauté the shallots, very finely chopped, for a couple of minutes. Dice the veal and add to the pan. Cook until slightly golden. Either chop the veal very finely by hand using a mezzaluna or chop in the food processor.
2. Put the onion and meat in a large mixing bowl or in the food processor, add all the remaining stuffing ingredients and knead together. Transfer to the fridge and leave for 10 minutes before using.

To make the dough

1. Pile the flour and salt on a large clean board or work surface and make a well in the centre.
2. Beat the eggs and then carefully and gradually add them to the well in the flour and work together to make a dough. Slowly add the milk as you work the dough. The dough should eventually become smooth. When it is smooth, roll it into a ball and leave for 10 minutes, covered.
3. Knead the dough again for 5–10 minutes on a floured surface until it is smooth and elastic. Leave covered for another 5 minutes.
4. Divide the dough into two, one piece slightly smaller than the other. The dough has now to be rolled out very thinly. See p. 110 for directions on how to roll out the dough.

To make the ravioli

1. Take the smaller sheet of pasta and place little heaps of stuffing, about 1 teaspoonful at a time, in rows approximately 2 in (5 cm) apart along the sheet of pasta.
2. When you have used up all the stuffing, lay the second sheet of pasta gently over the top. This sheet will mould itself over the lumps of stuffing, so that you can gently spread the lumps out with your fingers, pressing the dough together around the stuffing.
3. With a pasta cutting wheel, cut between each row of filling, first lengthwise and then across, so that you end up with little square parcels of pasta. To seal each parcel, gently press round the edges with the back of a fork.
4. Ravioli needs to be cooked in a generous quantity of boiling salted water in a large saucepan. The ravioli are cooked when they rise to the top. Do not try to cook too many at once.

TORTELLI DI ERBETTE
Tortelli *with Spinach and* Ricotta

This is a speciality of Parma; if you are in the region you should make a point of trying it.

To make the dough follow the directions for dough in the previous recipe. Roll out the dough and cut it into rectangles 2 × 3 in (5 × 6.5 cm), place the filling on one half and then fold the other half over the filling and press the edges to seal.

For the stuffing

8 OZ (225 G) COOKED
SPINACH

5 OZ (140 G) *RICOTTA*

1½ OZ (45 G) FRESHLY GRATED
PARMESAN

1 TEASPOON GRATED NUTMEG

SALT AND FRESHLY GROUND
BLACK PEPPER

2 LARGE EGGS

1 TABLESPOON OLIVE OIL

Mix all the ingredients together in a large bowl, leave for 10 minutes in the refrigerator and then use to fill the pasta, as explained above.

CAPPELLETTI IN BRODO
'Little Hats in Broth'

Cappelletti are savoury parcels of pasta made from squares of dough folded diagonally and then folded over into the shape of hats. The quantities given make about 80–100 *cappelletti*, enough for six people.

To make the dough, follow the directions on p. 137 for ravioli dough.

For the filling

1 OZ (30 G) BUTTER

2 TABLESPOONS OLIVE OIL

4 OZ (115 G) STEWING OR PIE VEAL, COOKED AND CHOPPED VERY FINELY

4 OZ (115 G) CHICKEN BREAST, BONED, COOKED AND CHOPPED VERY FINELY

1 SHALLOT

2 OZ (55 G) COOKED HAM OR MORTADELLA

2 EGGS

1 OZ (30 G) FRESHLY GRATED PARMESAN

SALT AND FRESHLY GROUND BLACK PEPPER

½ TEASPOON GRATED NUTMEG

To serve

4 PT (2.3 L) CHICKEN OR VEAL STOCK (PP. 59–60)

GRATED PARMESAN

To make the stuffing

1. Melt the butter in a shallow pan and add the oil. When it is hot add the veal, cook for 5 minutes and then add the chopped chicken breast and chopped shallot. Cook for a further 10 minutes.

2. Now chop the meat, either by hand or in the food processor, but not too finely – you do not want to make it into a 'mush'.

3. Put into a large mixing bowl with all the other ingredients and mix well together. Or mix in the food processor.

To make the cappelletti

1. Divide the dough into two pieces and cover one for use later. Roll out the other piece as thinly as possible, cut it into strips about 2 in (5 cm) wide, and then into squares.

2. Place just under half a teaspoon of the filling on a square of pasta and fold diagonally with the bottom edges projecting a little, and press to seal. Bend round the two ends of the long edge, with the point folded up, and press them firmly together.

3. When all the portions and filling have been used up, lay the *cappelletti* out on a flat clean surface to allow them to dry. Once dried, they will keep for about 3 days, or they can be frozen.

4. To cook the *cappelletti*, bring the stock to the boil and gently drop the *cappelletti* into it. When they rise to the top – about 3–5 minutes – they are cooked. Serve in soup plates with the broth and grated parmesan.

TORTE DI PASTA

In the shops of Parma and the surrounding region you are bound to notice the local speciality, *torta di pasta*: it is displayed in the huge flat trays in which it is baked and is sold by the portion. These *torte* are made from sheets of pasta, which are used to line the baking trays, and a savoury filling; a second sheet of pasta covers the filling.

Torte di pasta are quite easy to make at home once you have mastered the making of pasta. They are delicious and different – even in Italy they are not really known outside the region of Parma – and they make an excellent lunch or supper dish.

First you need to make the pasta: the quantities given below make enough pasta for two shallow baking trays 8 × 12 in (20 × 30 cm). The trays should have sides only ½–1 in (1.5–2.5 cm) high.

For the pasta

1 LB (450 G) STRONG WHITE PLAIN FLOUR
SALT
1 TEASPOON OLIVE OIL
2–3 EGGS (DEPENDING ON SIZE AND ON THE ABSORBENCY OF
    THE FLOUR)
4 TEASPOONS WARM MILK

1. Follow the basic recipe for making pasta (p. 108), adding the olive oil with the eggs.
2. Divide the dough into four pieces, or two pieces if you are using one very large baking tray. Lightly oil the trays.
3. Roll out the dough, not quite as thinly as when making ravioli, as the pasta sheets need to be substantial enough to

support the filling. Line the trays with the pasta, letting the sides overhang, and spread it generously with whichever filling you have chosen.

4. Roll out the remaining pieces of dough to cover the filling, again letting the pasta hang over the sides of the tray.

5. Make a small slit in the middle of the top. Take the two layers of pasta hanging over the sides, gently press them together and then twist them right round the edge (see diagram). Brush with beaten egg and bake at Mark 6 (400°F, 200°C) for approximately 20–30 minutes, until golden brown.

Spinach Filling

I LB (450 G) COOKED SPINACH
    WITH ALL THE WATER
    COMPLETELY SQUEEZED
    OUT, FINELY CHOPPED
SALT AND FRESHLY GROUND
    BLACK PEPPER
½ TEASPOON GRATED NUTMEG

3 EGGS
I OZ (30 G) FRESHLY GRATED
    PARMESAN
4 OZ (115 G) *RICOTTA*
    CHEESE
I TEASPOON OLIVE OIL

Mix all the ingredients together and use as a filling for the pies.

Potato and Leek Filling

2 LB (0.9 KG) BOILING POTATOES
I OZ (30 G) BUTTER
4 TABLESPOONS SINGLE CREAM
3 LEEKS
2 EGGS

1. Peel and boil the potatoes. Add the butter, cream and seasoning and purée or mash them until they are completely free from lumps.

2. Trim and slice the leeks. Fry until soft and add to the creamed potatoes with the eggs. Mix together well.

NB. Spinach can be added too – use 6 oz (170 g) cooked spinach for the quantities given.

GNOCCHI DI PATATE
Potato Gnocchi

Gnocchi – small dumplings – can be made without egg, but I find that when made with egg, the mixture is easier to handle and doesn't disintegrate in the water. *Gnocchi* is usually served as a first course, with a sauce. Romano red potatoes are particularly good for making *gnocchi*.

2 LB (0.9 KG) POTATOES
1–2 EGGS
6 OZ (170 G) PLAIN FLOUR
SALT

To serve

TOMATO (P. 93), *RAGÙ* (P. 101) OR GORGONZOLA (P. 124)
   SAUCE
FRESHLY GRATED PARMESAN

1. Boil the potatoes in their skins, or peel them first if you prefer. Drain; peel them while they are still warm if you have not already done so and then purée them immediately. If you have one, use a mouli-légumes to do this. Don't cheat – there must be no lumps at all!
2. Place the potato purée in a dish or on a floured wooden board, add almost all the flour and one egg, and knead until you have a smooth dough. The amount of flour and egg depends on the potatoes and you may find that you need to add the rest of the flour or some of the second egg. If you have decided to work on a board, add the egg and flour in a well in the potatoes.
3. When the dough is ready, shape it into long sausages about

1 in (2.5 cm) in diameter and cut each sausage into $\frac{3}{4}$ in (2 cm) lengths.

4. The next step sounds incredibly complicated, but it isn't really. Once you have acquired the knack you can make a heap of *gnocchi* before you know it.

Holding a long-pronged fork in one hand, take one piece of *gnocchi* in the other, press it – but not too hard – on the inside curve of the fork with your fingers, and then quickly flip it away (see diagram). The *gnocchi* will now have the marks of the prongs on one side. This is not only decorative, it also helps in the cooking of the *gnocchi* and makes it easier for the *gnocchi* to hold the delicious sauce you are going to serve with it!

5. To cook the *gnocchi*, boil 6–8 pt (3.4–4.5 l) water, add salt and carefully drop the *gnocchi* in, a few at a time. Soon they will start to come to the top of the pan; once they have done this let them cook for about another 10 seconds or so and then lift them out with a large slotted spoon. Place in a serving-dish and serve with tomato sauce, *ragù* or Gorgonzola sauce, and a little grated parmesan if you like.

GNOCCHI CON FAGIOLI
Gnocchi *with Borlotti Beans*

When I first tasted *gnocchi con fagioli*, in a restaurant just outside Piacenza, I thought it was quite delicious, so I devised this recipe for it.

I SMALL ONION, VERY FINELY CHOPPED

2 TABLESPOONS OLIVE OIL

4 OZ (115 G) DRIED BORLOTTI BEANS, WHICH HAVE BEEN SOAKED IN WATER OVERNIGHT

I RECIPE TOMATO SAUCE (P. 93)

SALT AND FRESHLY GROUND BLACK PEPPER

3 TABLESPOONS SINGLE CREAM

GNOCCHI (P. 144 – BUT MAKE THE GNOCCHI ABOUT HALF THE USUAL SIZE)

1. Cook the chopped onion in the oil for a few minutes until it is golden.
2. Add the beans, tomato sauce and seasoning, and bring to the boil. Simmer for 20 minutes. Add the cream.
3. Place the cooked *gnocchi* in a serving-dish and serve with the bean sauce.

GNOCCHI ALLA ROMANA

$1\frac{1}{2}$ PT (0.9 L) MILK
SALT
PEPPER
NUTMEG
6 OZ (170 G) ITALIAN
  SEMOLINA

3 OZ (85 G) GRATED
  PARMESAN
2 EGG YOLKS
2 OZ (55 G) BUTTER

1. Boil the milk in a heavy pan, and add the salt, pepper and nutmeg. Lower the heat and pour in the semolina very slowly in a thin trickle. Beat all the time with a whisk until you have a smooth, thick mixture.
2. Into this, mix half the cheese, the beaten egg yolks and the butter. Mix this thoroughly until everything is well blended.
3. Pour into a shallow, lightly buttered tin or dish and let it cool completely.
4. Set the oven to Mark 8 (450°F, 230°C).
5. When the semolina is cool cut it into rounds with a $1\frac{1}{2}$–2 in (4–5 cm) biscuit cutter or a glass.
6. Butter a rectangular ovenproof dish and lay the rounds in a single overlapping layer on the bottom of the dish. Sprinkle with the rest of the parmesan and dot with a little butter. Bake for about 15–20 minutes until it is golden brown and has a light crust on top.

GNOCCHI VERDI

To make green gnocchi, follow recipe for making Gnocchi di Patate and add 3 oz (85 g) cooked fresh spinach to the potato, flour and egg mixture.

RISOTTO

This versatile dish is one of my favourites, as it can be used for anything from a quick and simple lunch to the main course of a substantial meal. However, it has to be watched over and stirred often as it cooks and it must be served as soon as it is done; it cannot be kept warm until you are ready to eat and it cannot be partly cooked in advance. Risotto is therefore not really suitable for serving at a dinner party unless your guests don't mind sitting in the kitchen chatting while you get on with the cooking.

When you are making risotto, the basic technique described below should always be followed, using Arborio rice and a good stock. Keep the liquid simmering on the stove beside you, as it must always be hot when it is added to the rice. If you run out of stock before the risotto is cooked, you can finish with water. When it is ready, the risotto should hold together with a creamy texture; it should not be a sticky mass, nor should the grains of rice be swimming in a thin sauce.

BASIC RISOTTO

When cooking risotto it is important to judge the amount of liquid accurately. The knack is never to add too much liquid at once and always to add hot liquid. The amounts given are a guideline only – you may need to add more or less liquid according to the absorbency of the rice. Arborio rice should always be used; it will take about 25–30 minutes to cook.

To serve 4

1 OZ (30 G) BUTTER
1 TABLESPOON OLIVE OIL
1 SMALL ONION OR A COUPLE OF SHALLOTS
12 OZ (340 G) ARBORIO RICE
2–2¼ PT (1.1–1.2 L) STOCK (PP. 59–60)
SALT

1. Melt the butter in a heavy-bottomed pan large enough to take the expanded rice. Add the oil and the onion or shallots, chopped very finely. Sauté until the onion is slightly golden and glazed.
2. Add the rice and cook for about 2 minutes. At this point you must stir constantly to prevent the rice sticking.
3. Have the hot stock ready in a saucepan next to your rice. Add a ladleful of stock to the rice and stir. The rice will soon absorb the stock, and once it has done so – without becoming too dry – add another ladleful of stock and continue to let it cook until the stock has been almost completely absorbed. Stir constantly or the rice will stick to the pan. Continue adding the hot stock, slowly. Don't try and hurry the process by adding all the stock at once or turning up the heat – use an even medium heat throughout the process so that the rice bubbles away steadily.

After about 15–20 minutes taste a grain of rice, to see how much longer it needs to cook. If it is nearly ready you should not add much more liquid – the rice should be cooked, but still firm. When it is ready the risotto should have a creamy consistency and should go to the table still bubbling.

You may need to add salt, depending on the saltiness of the stock used.

RISOTTO CON FUNGHI SECCHI
Risotto with Dried Mushrooms

It is useful to keep this recipe in mind for when you have to make a meal unexpectedly, as it can be made entirely from ingredients from the store-cupboard.

To serve 4

1 OZ (30 G) DRIED ITALIAN
   PORCINI MUSHROOMS
2 PT (1.1 L) STOCK (PP. 59–60)
1 OZ (30 G) BUTTER
2 TABLESPOONS OLIVE OIL

1 SMALL ONION OR 2
   SHALLOTS
12 OZ (340 G) ARBORIO RICE
FRESHLY GROUND BLACK
   PEPPER
SALT

1. First, soak the mushrooms in ½ pt (275 ml) hot water for 20–30 minutes. Drain the mushrooms in a sieve lined with kitchen paper, and retain the water they were soaked in.
2. Have the stock ready in a saucepan, keeping hot. Melt the butter, add the oil and sauté the onions or shallots chopped finely until slightly golden.
3. Add the rice and cook for 2 minutes over a medium heat. Add one ladleful of stock, and when it has almost been absorbed add the mushrooms, roughly chopped. Now add just under a ladleful of the liquid from the mushrooms and season with pepper. Continue cooking as in basic risotto (p. 149), gradually adding the stock as the rice absorbs the liquid. Halfway through check for salt. Once cooked serve immediately.

Grated parmesan may be added at the end of the cooking if desired, but I feel this rather dominates the flavour of the mushrooms.

RISOTTO ALLA PARMIGIANA
Risotto with Parmesan

In Italy this risotto is sometimes served with sliced white truffles on top. Although very expensive they are quite a treat, and if you are able to buy truffles they will make the risotto very special.

To serve 4

1 OZ (30 G) BUTTER

1 TABLESPOON OLIVE OIL

1 SMALL ONION OR A COUPLE
   OF SHALLOTS

12 OZ (340 G) ARBORIO RICE

2¼ PT (1.2 L) STOCK (PP. 59–60)

SALT

3 OZ (85 G) PARMESAN –
   PARMIGIANO–REGGIANO, IF
   POSSIBLE

Follow the recipe for basic risotto (p. 149). About 5 minutes before the end of the cooking add the grated Reggiano.

As in basic risotto, check for salt, but don't leave it to the last minute – check after about the second or third ladleful of stock.

RISOTTO ALLA MARINARA
Seafood Risotto

After mastering the basic technique of making risotto, you can add whatever you feel like to flavour it.

Seafood is a wonderful accompaniment – prawns, fresh scampi, clams and mussels can all be added. This recipe uses tomato and prawns.

To serve 4

2 PT (1.1 L) STOCK (PP. 59–60)
8 LARGE UNCOOKED PRAWNS
1 SMALL ONION
12 OZ (340 G) ARBORIO RICE
1 OZ (30 G) BUTTER
2 TABLESPOONS OLIVE OIL

4 RIPE PLUM TOMATOES OR A
   14 OZ (400 G) TIN ITALIAN
   TOMATOES, DRAINED
SALT AND FRESHLY GROUND
   BLACK PEPPER
2 TABLESPOONS FINELY
   CHOPPED PARSLEY
1 CLOVE GARLIC, CRUSHED

1. Have the stock ready simmering.
2. Peel, clean, wash and slice the prawns and chop the onion very finely.
3. Cook the risotto in the usual way (see p. 149), using half the butter. About 5 minutes before the end brown the garlic and prawns in the rest of the butter, and add to the risotto with the tomatoes.

Risotto alla Milanese

To serve 4

2 PT (1.1 L) STOCK (PP. 59–60)	½ TEASPOON WHOLE SAFFRON, CHOPPED AND DISSOLVED IN
1 OZ (30 G) BUTTER	HOT WATER, OR USE ⅓
2 TABLESPOONS OLIVE OIL	TEASPOON POWDERED
1 SMALL ONION, FINELY CHOPPED	SAFFRON
1 OZ (30 G) *PROSCIUTTO CRUDO*	FRESHLY GROUND BLACK PEPPER
12 OZ (340 G) ARBORIO RICE	SALT
	2 TABLESPOONS FRESHLY GRATED PARMESAN

1. Have the hot stock ready simmering in a saucepan.
2. In a large, heavy pan melt the butter, add the olive oil, onion and *prosciutto*, and cook over a medium heat until the onion is slightly golden.
3. Add the rice, stir and cook for 2 minutes and then add a ladleful of hot broth and continue as in the basic risotto recipe (p. 149), adding the stock gradually as the rice absorbs it. When you have added just over half the stock, add the saffron and continue. Check the seasoning.
4. When the rice has cooked, add the grated parmesan and serve immediately.

RISOTTO CON RAGÙ
Risotto with Meat Sauce

This risotto can be very heavy and filling and is best served as a main course; if it is served as a first course then it should be followed by something very light and preferably without meat – perhaps some plain grilled fish and salad. In this recipe although 2 pt (1.1 l) liquid is used, approximately 1 pt (0.6 l) should be stock and the other water as I think meat stock and meat sauce is a little overpowering.

To serve 4

1 PT (0.6 L) STOCK (PP. 59–60)
2 LADLEFULS OF RAGÙ (P. 101)
1 OZ (30 G) BUTTER
1 TABLESPOON OIL
1 TABLESPOON CHOPPED ONION
12 OZ (340 G) ARBORIO RICE
2 OZ (55 G) FRESHLY GRATED PARMESAN

1. Dilute the stock with 1 pt (1.1 l) water; have the hot ragù ready.
2. Melt the butter in a heavy-bottomed pan over a medium heat and add the oil and the very finely chopped onion. Cook the onion for a few minutes or so until slightly golden.
3. Add the rice and stir constantly for 2 minutes. Add the ragù and cook until the rice has absorbed some of the liquid. Add a ladleful of stock, stirring continuously, and then proceed as for basic risotto – check for seasoning half way through.
4. When the rice is cooked mix in the grated parmesan and serve immediately.

RISOTTO CON SUGO DI POMIDORO
Risotto with Tomato Sauce

This recipe is made in exactly the same way as Risotto con Ragù, but we use one of the tomato sauces given on p. 93–6, and add fresh basil. If you want to make it a vegetarian dish, simply substitute a vegetable stock for the meat stock. Season with freshly ground black pepper.

I PT (0.6 L) VEGETABLE OR
  MEAT STOCK
½ PT (275 ML) TOMATO SAUCE
I OZ (30 G) BUTTER
I TABLESPOON OIL

I TABLESPOON ONION
  CHOPPED VERY FINELY
12 OZ (340 G) ARBORIO RICE
FRESHLY GROUND BLACK
  PEPPER
3–4 FRESH BASIL LEAVES

Follow the instructions opposite.

I Secondi Piatti
The Second Course

This chapter has been called 'The Second Course' because that is exactly what it is; in Italy the meat course does not dominate the meal as it does in England, and so it would be misleading to call it the 'main' course. Pasta, risotto, *gnocchi* or something of the kind is always served as a first course, before the meat or fish. (Obviously the size of the portions allows for the fact that there will be another course to come.) The meat may be accompanied by a vegetable dish, though not always, and it is often followed by a salad.

Veal or *vitellone*, which comes from older animals than our veal, is very popular, and I have given several traditional recipes for it. In some cases, chicken or turkey can be cooked in the same way — see, for example, the recipe for Cotolette alla Milanese, p. 167.

Fish, too, has an important place in the Italian diet, particularly in the south of Italy, where meat is eaten less often. Such is the variety and excellence of the fish available, from the long sea coast and from the lakes and rivers, that it is usually cooked quite simply, and served with a simple accompaniment.

Incidentally, if you are in Italy, do try to visit the local fish market, where there is sure to be a colourful display of fish and seafood in great variety. In particular, the fish market in Venice, on the Grand Canal near the Rialto bridge, is a sight not to be missed — but be sure to go early in the day.

ARROSTO DI VITELLO
Roast Veal

Roast veal is extremely popular in Italy and on Sunday most families have a dish of special pasta – home made ravioli perhaps – followed by a veal roast. It is not however, served in the same way as the British roast. The meat is the main attraction; it will be served with maybe a few fried potatoes or a crisp salad or some French beans – but not necessarily everything at once.

The cut of veal will depend on your butcher and where you live, as veal can be quite difficult to find in England and you may not have much choice – topside or shoulder are the usual cuts.

2–3 LB (1–1½ KG) JOINT OF VEAL
2 TABLESPOONS OLIVE OIL
1 CLOVE OF GARLIC, CRUSHED (OPTIONAL)
A COUPLE OF SPRIGS OF FRESH ROSEMARY
SALT AND FRESHLY GROUND BLACK PEPPER
1 OZ (30 G) BUTTER

1. Rinse the meat and dab dry. Place in a roasting tin and pour the olive oil over it. Rub the joint all over with the crushed garlic if you are using it. You can buy a garlic purée which consists solely of garlic and olive oil and is very good for this purpose.
2. Place the sprigs of rosemary over the veal and sprinkle with the salt and pepper.
3. Divide the butter into small pieces and dot them over the top of the veal.
4. Place the meat in a hot (Mark 8, 450°F, 230°C) oven for 10 minutes and then turn down to Mark 6 (400°F, 200°C). Cook

for about 2–2½ hours, turning from time to time until the meat is tender. Do not overcook the veal – juices should come from it when it is pierced with a fork.

You can cook the veal in foil if you prefer; if you do, remove the foil ½ hour before the end.

VITELLO TONNATO
Cold Veal with Tuna

This dish is attractive and delicious but it is quite substantial and is best served with something light such as a green salad. The veal joint can either be boiled with a few vegetables or roasted. When cold it is cut into slices and served with tuna sauce.

VEAL JOINT

For the tuna sauce

MAYONNAISE MADE FROM
½ PT (275 ML) LIGHT OLIVE
OIL, 2 LARGE EGG YOLKS
AND 2 TABLESPOONS FRESH
LEMON JUICE
3–4 ANCHOVY FILLETS
6 OZ (170 G) TIN ITALIAN TUNA
IN OLIVE OIL

1 TABLESPOON CAPERS
2 TABLESPOONS FRESH LEMON
JUICE
6 TABLESPOONS OLIVE OIL
1 TABLESPOON VERY FINELY
CHOPPED FRESH PARSLEY

To garnish

A FEW SPRIGS OF PARSLEY
A FEW SLICES OF LEMON

1. Either roast or boil the veal joint until tender. Allow to cool.
2. Make the mayonnaise following the directions on p. 88.
3. Place all the other ingredients in a blender and mix well. This can also be done by hand but the ingredients must be mixed thoroughly. Fold the purée carefully into the mayonnaise. Taste for salt – you may need a little depending on how salty the anchovies are.
4. Slice the cold veal (not too thinly) and place slightly overlapping on a serving-dish. Pour over the tuna sauce. Decorate with a few bits of parsley. Cover and refrigerate for at least 2–3 hours and serve with fresh lemon slices.

OSSO BUCO

Osso buco is shin of veal; the pieces should be about 2 in (5 cm) thick. This is a substantial dish and it is usually served with rice or spaghettini.

To serve 4

4 *OSSO BUCO* PIECES

PLAIN FLOUR FOR COATING THE
   MEAT

1 MEDIUM-SIZED ONION

A HANDFUL OF FRESH PARSLEY
   (DRIED WILL NOT DO)

2 OZ (55 G) BUTTER

6 TABLESPOONS COLD-PRESSED
   OLIVE OIL

JUICE AND ZEST OF 1 LEMON

$\frac{1}{2}$ WINEGLASS WHITE WINE

1 LARGE (22 OZ, 620 G) TIN
   OF ITALIAN PEELED
   TOMATOES, OR 2 LB FRESH
   TOMATOES, BOILED BRIEFLY
   AND PUT THROUGH A SIEVE

APPROXIMATELY 4 FL OZ (115
   ML) VEGETABLE STOCK OR
   WATER

1. Wash the meat and pat dry with kitchen paper. Coat the meat lightly with flour and shake off any excess.
2. Chop the onion and fresh parsley very finely.
3. In a heavy-bottomed pan large enough to hold all four pieces of veal comfortably, melt the butter and add the olive oil.
4. When the butter is hot, add the onion and cook for 2–3 minutes until soft; then add the parsley, the juice and zest of the lemon, and the wine.
5. Place each *osso buco* into the pan; the butter and oil in the pan should be hot enough to sizzle when the meat goes in. Cook the veal on a high heat for about 3 minutes on each side. Do not overcook at this stage or by the time the sauce is cooked, the meat will be dry. Add the seasoning.

6. Add the sieved tomatoes, bring to a brisk boil, give it a good stir, lower the heat and leave it to simmer for 20 minutes. Add the stock and simmer for another 20–30 minutes. Check the veal is just tender and taste for seasoning.

To accompany *osso buco* you can serve spaghettini or rice. This is a very hearty, filling dish and if you are serving anything before it, see that it is very light and does not contain meat.

SCALOPPINE ALLA MARSALA
Veal Scaloppine *with Marsala*

The most difficult part of this recipe is finding the *scaloppine*, for the veal must be cut across the grain of the meat. If the meat is not cut in this way, it will curl up when it is cooked. Some butchers seem to have a great deal of trouble with this particular cut of meat and it is therefore worthwhile seeking out a butcher who can cut *scaloppine* properly. Good-quality veal is expensive; pork is sometimes used instead, but is not a good substitute. The marsala used should be dry, not sweet.

To serve 4

1 LB (450 G) *SCALOPPINE*	1 SMALL ONION
2 OZ (55 G) PLAIN FLOUR	6 TABLESPOONS MARSALA
SALT AND FRESHLY GROUND	6 TABLESPOONS VEGETABLE
BLACK PEPPER	STOCK OR WATER
3 TABLESPOONS OLIVE OIL	2 OZ (55 G) BUTTER

1. Either get your butcher to beat out the veal or do it yourself by placing the veal between two sheets of greaseproof paper and beating until thin. Cut into pieces roughly 2 in (5 cm) square – they do not have to be uniform.
2. Have the flour seasoned with the salt and pepper on a large plate and dip each piece of veal into the flour so that both sides are coated, shaking off any excess. Do not do this until you are ready to use the meat.
3. Melt half the butter in a large shallow pan and add the oil. Cut the onion into quarters and use to flavour the oil – cook the onion until it has softened and gone slightly golden and then remove it from the pan. Add the *scaloppine* and cook for about 15–20 seconds on each side.

4. Add the marsala and leave on a medium heat for 10 seconds or so; then stand back and ignite it. My mother-in-law is marvellous at this: she quickly tilts the pan with great expertise and lets the gas flame ignite the sauce. If the alcohol is very hot the flames will be quite high, but don't panic – they will soon die down. (It is a good idea to have a lid ready to cover the pan in case of emergency.) Now add the water or stock and butter and boil briskly for 5 minutes; then turn down the heat and cook for a further 5 minutes, turning the *scaloppine* once or twice.

Tiny fresh peas put in for the last 5 minutes are delicious with the *scaloppine*.

COTOLETTE ALLA MILANESE

Cotolette are veal *scaloppine* dipped in egg, coated in fresh breadcrumbs and cooked quickly in hot oil. Chicken or turkey breasts can be cooked in the same way.

To serve 4–6

2–3 *SCALOPPINE* PER PERSON
2 WHOLE EGGS
6 OZ (170 G) FRESH BREADCRUMBS
OLIVE OIL FOR COOKING
SALT
LEMON WEDGES

1. Pound the *scaloppine* between two sheets of greaseproof paper with a rolling-pin.
2. Beat the eggs well in a shallow dish and have the breadcrumbs ready on a plate.
3. Dip each piece of veal into the beaten egg and then into the breadcrumbs. Make sure they are well coated and shake off any excess. Place the prepared *scaloppine* on a plate. Do not pile them on top of each other if you are not going to use them immediately.
4. Using a shallow frying-pan, pour in enough oil to come about ¼ in (6 mm) up the side of the pan. Heat the oil until it is very hot. Drop in as many *cotolette* as possible. (They should sizzle as they go in – if they do not the oil is not hot enough.)

When they are golden brown and crispy on one side, turn and cook the other side. The process is very quick – be careful not to overcook the *cotolette*. When they are golden lift out immediately on to absorbent kitchen paper and dab lightly. Sprinkle on a little salt and serve immediately with the lemon wedges.

Peperonata (p. 216) goes very well with *cotolette alla milanese*.

SCALOPPINE DI VITELLO AL LIMONE
Veal scaloppine with lemon

To serve 4

1 LB (450 G) VEAL *SCALOPPINE*
2½ OZ (70 G) PLAIN FLOUR
SALT AND FRESHLY GROUND
   BLACK PEPPER
3 TABLESPOONS OLIVE OIL
2 OZ (55 G) BUTTER

4 TABLESPOONS FRESH LEMON
   JUICE
LEMON SLICES FOR
   DECORATION
2 TABLESPOONS FRESH PARSLEY

Follow the recipe for Scaloppine Marsala, steps 1, 2 and 3, for the preparation of the meat. Heat the oil in a pan and cook the *scaloppine* for about 20 seconds on each side.

When the *scaloppine* are browned add the lemon juice and butter, scraping the bottom of the pan with a wooden spoon. Cook for about 2 minutes and then add the fresh parsley. Stir and cook for a further minute, and then serve.

BISTECCA ALLA FIORENTINA
Grilled Steak

A Florentine steak is a huge piece of meat cut from the rib. It is wonderfully tender and full of flavour, and is often grilled or cooked over a charcoal fire. If you order one in Italy, it will be served with a wedge of lemon, without vegetables, and this really is the best way to eat it.

In Italy the Florentine steak is truly delicious – it is made from the best beef in Italy, from the Chianina breed of cattle raised in the Val di Chiana. In England we must make do with a T-bone steak, grilled and served with wedges of lemon. A green salad and ripe tomatoes dressed with your best olive oil and wine vinegar go well afterwards.

POLPETTONE DELLA BISNONNA
Great-grandmother's Stuffed Beef

1½ OZ (45 G) BUTTER

10 OZ (285 G) COOKED
SPINACH

1 LARGE EGG YOLK

6 OZ (170 G) *RICOTTA*
CHEESE

2 TABLESPOONS GRATED
PARMESAN

SALT AND FRESHLY GROUND
BLACK PEPPER

A PINCH OF NUTMEG

1 THICK SLICE *MORTADELLA*,
ABOUT 6 OZ (170 G)

1½ LB (0.7 KG) FILLET OF BEEF,
OR SIMILAR, FLATTENED

A SMALL GLASS DRY WHITE
WINE

½ PT (275 ML) CHICKEN STOCK

1. Melt the butter and warm the cooked spinach; then mix in the egg yolk, cheese (*ricotta* and parmesan) and seasoning.

2. Place the slice of *mortadella* on the meat and spread the spinach mixture over it. Carefully roll up into a large sausage shape and tie securely with string in the middle and at both ends.

3. In a large shallow pan melt some butter and brown the meat lightly all over. Add the wine and a ladleful of stock. Cover the pan and simmer for 2 hours, adding a little stock now and again. After 2 hours turn off the heat and leave for 10 minutes; then remove and slice.

This dish can be eaten hot or cold.

STRACOTTO AL BAROLO
Fillet of Pork in Barolo

This is quite an expensive dish, but it makes a very good main course for a special occasion. Barolo is a strong, full-bodied red wine from the foothills of the Apennines in Piedmont. You could make this dish with another strong red wine, but it would not have the special flavour of Barolo.

4 OZ (115 G) *PANCETTA*

1½–2 LB (0.7–0.9 KG) FILLET
OF PORK

2 OZ (55 G) BUTTER

1 MEDIUM-SIZED ONION

2 OZ (55 G) FLOUR

2 STICKS CELERY

1 CARROT, SLICED

1 LADLEFUL STOCK

¾ BOTTLE OF BAROLO WINE

1 CLOVE OF GARLIC, CRUSHED

FRESH ROSEMARY

A FEW BAY LEAVES

A FEW BLACK PEPPERCORNS

SALT

1. Tie the *pancetta* securely to the meat.
2. Melt the butter in a large casserole and lightly brown the chopped onion. Dip the piece of pork into the flour, shaking off any excess. Gently brown it all over for a few minutes in the pan with the onion.
3. Dice the celery and carrot and add to the pan with the rest of the ingredients. Bring quickly to the boil and then simmer very slowly for 2 hours.
4. When the meat is cooked, place it on a carving dish and blend the juices in the pan, which will now be much reduced.
5. Slice the meat and pour the sauce over it.

SPALLA DI AGNELLO FARCITA
Stuffed Shoulder of Lamb

4 OZ (115 G) *PANCETTA*
2 TABLESPOONS FRESH PARSLEY
1 CLOVE OF GARLIC, CRUSHED
A FEW FRESH BAY LEAVES
SALT AND FRESHLY GROUND
 BLACK PEPPER

2 LB (0.9 KG) SHOULDER OF
 LAMB, BONED
2 OZ (55 G) BUTTER
½ GLASS DRY WHITE WINE
1 LADLEFUL STOCK

1. Dice the *pancetta* and mix with the chopped parsley, garlic, bay leaves and seasoning.
2. Spread the meat with this mixture, roll up and tie securely.
3. Melt the butter in a pan with a lid and brown the meat lightly. Pour in the wine and simmer. When the wine has reduced, add the stock, cover and simmer for 1 hour.
4. Allow the meat to rest for at least 10 minutes before serving.

COSTOLETTE D'AGNELLO
Lamb Cutlets with Rosemary

Italians are very fond of lamb with rosemary. This is a typical recipe.

OLIVE OIL
I TABLESPOON FRESH LEMON JUICE
$\frac{1}{2}$ CLOVE OF GARLIC, FINELY CRUSHED
SALT AND FRESHLY GROUND BLACK PEPPER
A FEW SPRIGS OF FRESH ROSEMARY
4 LAMB CUTLETS

1. Mix together the oil, lemon juice, garlic and seasoning. If you like you can chop the rosemary very finely and mix it with the oil too.
2. Brush both sides of the cutlets with the mixture and refrigerate for 30 minutes.
3. If you did not mix the rosemary with the oil in stage 1, lay the sprigs over the rack of the grill pan, put the cutlets on top and cook under a medium grill until crisp outside and pink inside.

FRITTO MISTO

If you are in Italy you will no doubt come across this dish on restaurant menus. *Fritto misto* means 'mixed fry' and it is usually a mixture of meats such as veal escalopes and calves' liver and brains, and vegetables like artichokes, asparagus, mushrooms and courgettes . . . you can choose whatever you like. Each food is dipped in flour or breadcrumbs and then fried in oil. It must be served as soon as it is cooked.

FEGATO ALLA VENEZIANA
Calves' Liver and Onions

Fegato alla Veneziana is made with calves' liver cut into very thin slices.

To serve 4

1½ LB (0.7 KG) CALVES' LIVER
4 MEDIUM-SIZED ONIONS
½ OZ (15 G) BUTTER
3 TABLESPOONS OLIVE OIL
SALT AND FRESHLY GROUND BLACK PEPPER

1. Trim the liver and cut into small, very thin slices – try to keep them uniform in size.
2. Slice the onions thinly. Melt the butter in a frying-pan, add the oil and cook the onions until pale and very slightly golden; this will take about 10–12 minutes. Remove the onions from the pan but do not throw away the oil and butter.
3. Heat up the pan again, add the liver and season well. Cook over a high heat until the liver becomes brownish. This only takes a few minutes – do not overcook. Put the onions back into the pan, cook for another few seconds to warm the onions again and then serve immediately.

FEGATO DI VITELLO AL MARSALA
Calves' Liver with Marsala

To serve 4

8–12 OZ (225–340 G) CALVES' LIVER
SALT AND FRESHLY GROUND BLACK PEPPER
PLAIN FLOUR
1 OZ (30 G) BUTTER
3 TABLESPOONS DRY MARSALA
½ TEACUP CHICKEN OR VEGETABLE STOCK

1. Cut the liver into small slices, season and flour lightly.
2. Melt the butter in a shallow heavy pan and add the liver and the marsala. Cook for a couple of minutes on each side.
3. Add the stock and simmer for 10 minutes.

POLLO ARROSTO CON ROSMARINO
Roast Chicken with Rosemary

ROASTING CHICKEN (PREFERABLY FREE–RANGE)
2 TABLESPOONS OLIVE OIL
1 CLOVE OF GARLIC, CRUSHED (OPTIONAL)
SALT AND FRESHLY GROUND BLACK PEPPER
A FEW SPRIGS OF FRESH ROSEMARY OR EQUIVALENT DRIED
   ROSEMARY

1. Preheat the oven to Mark 6 (400°F, 200°C). Clean the chicken and dry well.
2. Rub the chicken all over with the oil, and the garlic if you are using it. Season with the salt and pepper. Scatter half the rosemary over the chicken and put the other half into the cavity. Put the chicken on an oiled roasting tin, put it in the oven and cook according to the size of the chicken, turning and basting occasionally. (A medium-sized chicken will take about an hour.)

POLLO ARROSTO CON SPINACI
Roast Chicken Stuffed with Spinach

This is a good way of giving roast chicken more flavour, and the green of the spinach also adds colour.

I ROASTING CHICKEN
I LB (450 G) SPINACH
I SMALL ONION
3 OZ (85 G) FRESH
   BREADCRUMBS
2 EGGS

3 FL OZ (85 ML) MILK
NUTMEG
FRESHLY GROUND BLACK
   PEPPER
2 TABLESPOONS OLIVE OIL

1. Set the oven to Mark 6 (400°F, 200°C).
2. Clean, wash and dry the chicken with kitchen paper.
3. Wash the spinach at least three times and remove any tough stalks. Leave the spinach wet and place in a saucepan on a medium heat; shake and move round until the spinach has reduced, then drain and place between two plates to squeeze out all the water.
4. Chop the spinach and onion very finely and put into a large mixing bowl. Add the breadcrumbs, eggs, milk, nutmeg and pepper. Mix thoroughly, add half the olive oil and mix again. If you have a food processor, it will do this for you all at once.
5. Rub the chicken with the rest of the olive oil and sprinkle lightly with salt and pepper.
6. Stuff the chicken with the spinach mixture. Wrap loosely in foil, place in a roasting tin and cook until done (the cooking time will vary according to the size of the chicken – a medium-sized chicken will take about an hour) turning occasionally; remove the foil 30 minutes before the end.

POLLO CON FUNGHI
Chicken with Mushrooms

The wonderful flavour of dried *porcini* mushrooms makes this chicken dish really special.

To serve 4

1 OZ (30 G) DRIED *PORCINI* MUSHROOMS	¼ PT (150 ML) CHICKEN STOCK
4 FRESH CHICKEN BREASTS	SALT AND FRESHLY GROUND BLACK PEPPER
1 OZ (30 G) BUTTER	
2 TABLESPOONS OLIVE OIL	6 TABLESPOONS SINGLE CREAM

1. Soak the mushrooms in hot water for 30 minutes. You will need about a teacup of water.
2. Wash the chicken breasts, pat dry and put to one side. Drain the mushrooms through a sieve lined with kitchen paper, retaining the water, and then chop them coarsely.
3. In a heavy-bottomed pan large enough to hold all four chicken breasts in a single layer, melt the butter and add the oil. Now add the mushrooms and cook for 1 minute.
4. Place the chicken in the pan and cook on each side for 2 minutes. Pour in the chicken stock and continue to cook on a medium heat for 15 minutes, adding about half of the liquid retained from the mushrooms. Check for seasoning – if the stock is salty you may not need to add extra salt.
5. After about 15 minutes the stock should have reduced. Check that the chicken is cooked by piercing with a fork – the juices should run clear. If the stock has reduced sufficiently, add the cream and cook for a further minute.

Serve immediately with rice or Potate con Rosmarino (p. 220).

POLLO CON ROSMARINO
Chicken Pieces and Potatoes Cooked with Fresh Rosemary

This is a very simple dish, but potatoes and chicken cooked in this way have a delicious flavour.

To serve 4

1 MEDIUM-SIZED FRESH CHICKEN (CUT INTO SECTIONS)
3 LB (1.4 KG) POTATOES
2 OZ (55 G) BUTTER
4 TABLESPOONS OLIVE OIL
2–3 SPRIGS OF FRESH ROSEMARY
SALT

1. Joint the chicken, wash the pieces and dry with kitchen paper.
2. Peel the potatoes and cut into quarters if the potatoes are large or halve them if they are small. Dry on paper.
3. In a large shallow pan melt the butter and add the olive oil and rosemary. When the butter and oil are hot, add the chicken pieces and cook on quite a high heat for about 3 minutes, turning the meat to seal and brown it quickly.
4. Add the potatoes and salt. Continue cooking, turning the chicken and potatoes all the time, for about 40 minutes on a low heat until the meat and potatoes have cooked and browned. To check that the chicken is cooked pierce with a fork – the juices should run clear. Remove the rosemary and serve with a green vegetable or salad and fresh crusty bread.

COTECHINO CON FAGIOLI
Cotechino with Beans

Cotechino is a strongly-flavoured boiling sausage made from pork, a speciality of the Emilia-Romagna. You will see them strung up with salami and other sausages in Italian food shops.

I *COTECHINO* SAUSAGE
6 OZ (170 G) BORLOTTI BEANS
I ONION
I TABLESPOON OLIVE OIL
14 OZ (395 G) TIN OF PEELED TOMATOES
SALT AND FRESHLY GROUND BLACK PEPPER

1. Soak the sausage and beans overnight in a bowl of cold water. Bring about 4 pints (2.3 l) water to the boil in a large pan, put in the sausage and let it simmer very slowly for 3 hours.
2. Boil the beans for 1 hour and then drain them.
3. About an hour before the end of the *cotechino* cooking time start preparing the sauce. Chop the onion finely and cook in the oil until pale golden. Add the beans and the sieved tomatoes, season, bring to a brisk boil and simmer 1 hour.

When the sausage is cooked, cut it into thick slices and serve with the sauce.

POLENTA CON CONIGLIO
Polenta with Rabbit

This is a recipe to make on a cold rainy winter day when you feel like cooking in a warm kitchen with appetizing smells rising from the pan.

I RABBIT, JOINTED

1–2 GLASSES DRY WHITE WINE

FRESH PARSLEY OR THYME

I MEDIUM ONION

2 LEEKS

2 CARROTS

I STICK CELERY

4 OZ (115 G) CULTIVATED FIELD MUSHROOMS OR 2–3 DRY *PORCINI*

6 PLUM TOMATOES

I OZ (30 G) BUTTER

3 TABLESPOONS COLD-PRESSED OLIVE OIL

½ PT (275 ML) VEGETABLE STOCK

SALT

2 TABLESPOONS SINGLE CREAM (OPTIONAL)

12 OZ (340 G) COARSE *POLENTA*

1. The rabbit should be marinated for 3–4 hours, or overnight if possible. Chop it into smallish pieces and place it in a large shallow dish. Pour over the wine, sprinkle with the fresh thyme or parsley, cover and put into the fridge.

2. When you are ready to cook, prepare the vegetables – chop the onion and slice the leeks, carrots and celery diagonally. Slice the mushrooms and cut the tomatoes in quarters.

3. Everything is now going to be cooked together very slowly, so you need a heavy-bottomed pan which is not too deep but is quite wide. Melt the butter in the pan with the olive oil. Add the onion and leek and cook for 2 minutes. Now remove the rabbit from the marinade and brown it quickly all over in the pan with the onion and leek – this should take about 5 minutes. Add the rest of the vegetables. Cook for 10 minutes

and then pour in the stock. Add salt if necessary. Bring to the boil and simmer for 1 hour. Just before serving add the cream.

About 40 minutes before the end of the cooking time start to prepare the *polenta* (p. 204).

POLENTA WITH SAUSAGES

Luganega is a mild pork sausage which is widely available in Italy; it can bought at specialist food shops in Britain.

To serve 4

1 SMALL ONION
4 TABLESPOONS OLIVE OIL
4 ITALIAN SAUSAGES (LUGANEGA)
6 FRESH PLUM TOMATOES OR AN 8 OZ (225 G) TIN OF
    TOMATOES
SALT AND FRESHLY GROUND BLACK PEPPER
12 OZ (340 G) COARSE *POLENTA*

1. Chop the onion finely and cook in the olive oil until golden; then add the sausages and cook for 10–15 minutes, turning them so that they cook evenly.
2. Chop the tomatoes either fresh or tinned and add to the sausages; taste and season. Stir, cover and simmer for 30 minutes – if the tomatoes reduce too much, add a little water.
3. While the sausages are cooking make the *polenta* (p. 204). When the polenta is ready pour it into a serving-dish, place the sausages and sauce in the middle, and serve.

BACCALÀ
Salt Fish

Baccalà is salt fish, usually cod, large haddock or hake. In Britain it is generally cod, which is sold dried and has to be soaked for at least 48 hours. In Italy you can buy *baccalà* which has already been soaked and is ready to use. *Baccalà* used to be a common dish on Fridays in Italy, but it is now becoming quite rare.

In Britain, people still shy away from it because of the soaking and preparation involved but it has an unusual flavour, quite different from that of ordinary cod, and is well worth a try.

Baccalà is sold in long pieces in specialist shops and is extremely difficult to cut while dry. Normally the shop will cut the fish into more manageable pieces for you.

Baccalà must be soaked for at least 48 hours with several changes of water. For the last hour or so it should be left under cold running water. Then place it in milk for another 2 hours. Pull off the skin, remove all bones and cut into small chunks. Cook it in the sauce described for Osso Buco (p. 163).

GAMBERONI
Prawns

Prawns cooked in this way are simply delicious, served as an *antipasto*, first course or main course with a crisp green salad with tomatoes. Buy large uncooked prawns.

6 TABLESPOONS OLIVE OIL
1 SQUEEZED LEMON
SALT AND FRESHLY GROUND BLACK PEPPER
2 TABLESPOONS FINELY CHOPPED FRESH PARSLEY
PRAWNS
2 CLOVES OF GARLIC, CRUSHED

1. Mix the olive oil, lemon juice, seasoning and parsley together in a bowl.
2. Wash the prawns but leave them unpeeled. Mix the prawns into the marinade and leave for 30 minutes.
3. Remove the prawns from the marinade, place on a baking tray, put under a medium hot grill and cook for about 5 minutes on each side, brushing occasionally with the marinade.
  Serve immediately.

Alternatively, the prawns may be fried in olive oil with a little garlic.

RED MULLET WITH ROSEMARY

This may sound a little boring but is extremely tasty; the secret is to buy really good fresh red mullet. It goes very well after a heavy pasta course and is simple to prepare.

I RED MULLET PER PERSON
3 TABLESPOONS OLIVE OIL
A FEW SPRIGS OF FRESH ROSEMARY
SALT AND FRESHLY GROUND BLACK PEPPER.

1. Clean and scale the fish, and pat dry.
2. Heat the oil in a shallow pan large enough to hold all the fish. Add the fish, rosemary and seasoning and cook for about 3–5 minutes on each side until crisp and brown.

PASTICCIO DI SARDINE
Baked Sardines

1–1½ LB (450–680 G) FRESH
SARDINES

2 OZ (55 G) FRESH GRATED
BREADCRUMBS

FRESH CHOPPED PARSLEY

½ GARLIC CLOVE, CRUSHED

SALT AND FRESHLY GROUND
BLACK PEPPER

LEMON JUICE

2 OZ (55 G) BUTTER

2 EGGS

1 TEACUP MILK

1. Remove the heads of the sardines; slit them along the belly, open out and remove the backbones.

2. Working from the centre, arrange half the sardines, opened out flat, in a large, round, heatproof dish which has been lightly oiled.

3. In a bowl mix together the breadcrumbs, fresh parsley, garlic and seasoning, and spread this over the sardines. Sprinkle with the lemon juice and dab with small pieces of butter, and then finish off with the rest of the sardines.

4. Beat together the milk and eggs and pour over the fish. Add another few pieces of butter and place in moderate oven (Mark 5, 375°F, 190°C) for 30 minutes until lightly browned.

DOVER SOLE

This is a very simple and quick way of preparing and cooking Dover sole; serve with some simple vegetables, or a warm salad such as Insalata di Zuccini e Fagiolini (p. 232) or Insalata di Fagiolini (p. 227).

To serve 4

8 FILLETS OF DOVER SOLE
PLAIN FLOUR TO COAT THE FISH
SALT AND FRESHLY GROUND BLACK PEPPER
OLIVE OIL
1 TABLESPOON CHOPPED PARSLEY, PLUS A FEW EXTRA SPRIGS
1 LEMON, SQUEEZED

1. Wash and trim the fillets, leaving the fish wet.
2. Put some flour seasoned with salt and pepper in a shallow dish. Take one fillet of sole at a time and dip it in the flour, pressing the fish down into the flour so that it sticks. Repeat with the rest of the fish.
3. Heat the olive oil in a shallow frying-pan – it should be about ½ in (1 cm) deep. Add a few sprigs of parsley. When the oil is hot add the fillets, all at once if your pan is large enough. Cook for about 1 minute on each side.
4. Lift the fish out of the oil, dab with absorbent kitchen paper, sprinkle with the lemon juice and garnish with parsley.

DOVER SOLE WITH CREAM AND MARSALA

To serve 4

8 FILLETS OF DOVER SOLE
PLAIN FLOUR FOR COATING
1 OZ (30 G) BUTTER
3 FL OZ (85 ML) FISH STOCK
   OR WATER

1 TABLESPOON CHOPPED
   PARSLEY
3 TABLESPOONS MARSALA
4 TABLESPOONS SINGLE CREAM

1. Trim and wash the fillets of sole, dab with kitchen paper and coat very lightly in flour.
2. Melt the butter in a large shallow pan, add the fish and cook for 30 seconds on each side.
3. Add the fish stock and chopped parsley, turn up the heat and let it boil for about 2 minutes.
4. Turn the heat down again and add the marsala and cream. Cook for another 2 minutes, taste for salt and serve immediately.

SOGLIOLE CON PREZZEMOLO E POMIDORI
Sole with Parsley and Tomato Purée

8 FILLETS OF DOVER SOLE
GARLIC PURÉE OR A CLOVE OF GARLIC, CRUSHED
TOMATO PURÉE
2 TABLESPOONS FRESH PARSLEY, VERY FINELY CHOPPED

1. Take each fillet of sole and rub very lightly with a little garlic purée and spread with a little tomato purée.
2. Sprinkle each fillet with the fresh parsley, roll up and tie.
3. Place in an oiled heatproof dish and bake in a medium oven (Mark 4, 350°F, 180°C) for 20 minutes.

The fish can be surrounded by a little tomato sauce if desired.

Trota Marinata
Grilled Marinated Trout

Trout is very popular in Italy but more often than not is cooked very simply, either grilled, baked, fried or boiled, or on charcoal. In this recipe the trout is marinated for half an hour and then grilled.

To serve 4

4 TROUT (NOT TOO BIG)
6 TABLESPOONS OLIVE OIL
3 TABLESPOONS FRESH LEMON JUICE
SALT AND FRESHLY GROUND BLACK PEPPER
2 TABLESPOONS FINELY CHOPPED FRESH PARSLEY

1. Wash, clean and scale the trout, and dab with kitchen paper. Score the trout diagonally down each side without cutting into the flesh.
2. Mix together the oil, lemon juice, seasoning and parsley, and leave the trout in this marinade for 30 minutes, turning occasionally.
3. Place the trout on a lightly oiled, heatproof, rectangular dish or tray and grill for about 10 minutes on each side, brushing occasionally with the remainder of the marinade.

TROTA AI FERRI
Fried Trout

4 FRESH TROUT
PLAIN FLOUR TO COAT THE FISH
SALT AND FRESHLY GROUND BLACK PEPPER
1 CLOVE OF GARLIC
1 TABLESPOON FRESH PARSLEY, FINELY CHOPPED
8 TABLESPOONS OLIVE OIL

1. Wash, clean and scale the trout. Dab with kitchen paper and score diagonally down each side. Dip into seasoned flour and shake off the excess.
2. Crush the garlic clove and chop the parsley, and add to the olive oil in a large frying-pan. When the oil is hot add the trout and cook for approximately 5 minutes on each side until cooked.

Lunch and Supper Dishes

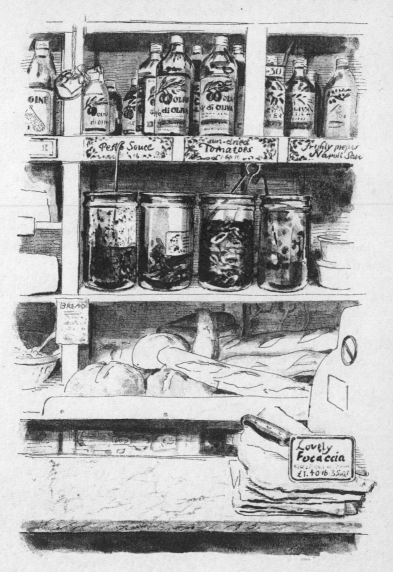

PIZZA

If you are looking for a cheap, filling and tasty meal when you are in Italy, you need look no farther than a *pizzeria*.

The pizza makes such a convenient snack meal that it has travelled to Britain and across the Atlantic to America; there is also a traditional local version, called *pissaladière*, in the area around Nice. In each country it has been adapted to suit the local ingredients and tastes. In Italy, the pizza base is quite thin, the garnish light and delicious, a far cry from most pizzas sold in Britain.

Many people seem to think that pizza is difficult to make and that it will take hours in the kitchen kneading and preparing the dough. This is a pity – it may take a couple of tries before you get it right, but once you have acquired the knack it is quite easy and gives a great sense of achievement.

When we are staying in Italy, Zia Antonia will often make a huge pizza, lightly topped with fresh tomatoes, fresh basil, mozzarella cheese and maybe a few anchovies – delicious! Because normal household ovens are not usually hot enough, Italians often wrap their pizzas in an old tablecloth with the corners knotted together and take it to the local baker's to be cooked.

PIZZA NAPOLETANA

If possible, try to buy fresh origano for this pizza; if you can't get origano, fresh basil will do.

To serve 2–3

Pizza dough

½ OZ (15 G) FRESH YEAST
½ LB (225 G) PLAIN FLOUR
SALT

Topping

OLIVE OIL
4–6 FRESH TOMATOES (DEPENDING ON SIZE)
4–6 OZ (115–170 G) FRESH ITALIAN *MOZZARELLA*
ABOUT 8 ANCHOVY FILLETS
FRESH ORIGANO OR FRESH BASIL

1. Add a little tepid water to the yeast and stir until dissolved.
2. Pile the flour on a large wooden board, make a well in the centre and add the yeast and a scant teaspoon of salt.
3. Carefully fold the flour over the yeast.
4. Add enough warm water (about 4–6 fl oz, 115–170 ml) to make a stiff but pliable dough. If you find the dough is too stiff, add a little more water.
5. Knead the dough with the palm of your hand, pressing and pushing it away from you – this should take about 10 to 15 minutes. When the dough is smooth and elastic and much lighter, shape it into a ball, cover with a clean cloth and a sheet of polythene and leave in a warm place on a lightly floured plate or dish until it has doubled in size. This will take

about 1–2 hours, depending on the temperature – it rises faster when the kitchen is warm.

6. Set the oven to its highest temperature.

7. When the dough has risen, roll it out on a floured board to the shape you require, either circular or rectangular, and about ¼ in (6 mm) thick. This quantity will make either one large pizza or two smaller ones.

8. Prepare your baking tins by rubbing them over with a little olive oil. Place the dough in the tins and cover with the skinned and chopped tomatoes and the cheese and anchovies. Season and sprinkle over the origano or basil and a few drops of oil.

9. Place in the oven and bake for 10 minutes on the highest temperature; then reduce the temperature to Mark 7 (425°F, 220°C) and bake for a further 10 minutes.

PIZZA ALLA FRANCESCANA

PIZZA DOUGH
3 OZ (85 G) COOKED HAM OR 2 OZ (55 G) PARMA HAM
3 TOMATOES, PEELED AND CHOPPED
2 OZ (55 G) *MOZZARELLA*
2 OZ (55 G) BEL PAESE
3 OZ (85 G) MUSHROOMS
OLIVE OIL

Make the dough as for Pizza Napoletana (p. 198). Cover with pieces of ham, the chopped tomatoes and the sliced cheese and mushrooms. Sprinkle a few drops of olive oil over it and cook as before.

Pizza Margherita

This pizza displays the colours of the Italian flag, red, green and white.

PIZZA DOUGH
4–6 FRESH TOMATOES, PEELED AND CHOPPED
6 OZ (170 G) FRESH ITALIAN *MOZZARELLA*
2 TEASPOONS FRESH CHOPPED BASIL
OLIVE OIL

Prepare the dough as for Pizza Napoletana (p. 198). Cover it with slices of tomato and cheese and sprinkle the basil and oil over it. Cook as before.

Pizza alla Siciliana

PIZZA DOUGH
4–6 FRESH TOMATOES, PEELED AND CHOPPED
10 ANCHOVY FILLETS
SALT AND PEPPER
BLACK OLIVES, STONED AND CHOPPED
OLIVE OIL

Proceed as for Pizza Napoletana (p. 198).

FOCACCIA

Focaccia is a flattish, crusty bread, seen in most bakers' and bars in Italy. The aroma of it as it cooks early in the morning will send you rushing into the baker's. It is made from pizza dough, usually just sprinkled with olive oil and salt and then baked. In some parts of Liguria stoned olives are pressed into the dough before it is baked.

To make *focaccia* prepare a normal pizza dough (p. 198), but roll it out to about ¾ in (2 cm) thick. Place it on a well-oiled baking-tray, coat it lightly with olive oil, sprinkle with coarse salt and bake it at Mark 7 (425°F, 220°C) for 30–40 minutes.

POLENTA

Polenta is maize flour. You can buy it finely ground or coarsely ground, and you can also get pre-cooked *polenta*. The coarsely ground *polenta* is more suitable for the recipes given here. *Polenta* may look like a thick yellow porridge, but it is delicious; it can be served with stewed or roast meat; it can also be eaten with cheese and butter or with Italian sausages. In northern Italy it is cooked in a large copper pot kept specially for the purpose, but any heavy-bottomed pan will do.

12 OZ (340 G) *POLENTA*
A SCANT TABLESPOON SALT

1. In a large heavy-bottomed pan bring 3 pt (1.7 l) water to the boil; when the water has boiled add the salt and turn down the heat so that the water is simmering gently.
2. Have a long-handled wooden spoon ready for stirring with. Add the *polenta* to the water very slowly, in a fine stream, stirring all the time. If you add it too quickly you will end up with a mass of lumps.
3. When all the *polenta* has been added continue cooking, stirring frequently, for 25 minutes. The *polenta* should now be coming away from the sides of the pan.
4. When it is ready, turn the *polenta* out on to a wooden board or into a shallow dish and serve immediately.

POLENTA AL BURRO E FORMAGGIO
Polenta *with Butter and Cheese*

This is a very simple way of serving *polenta*. It makes a tasty lunch or supper dish.

12 OZ (340 G) COARSE *POLENTA*
SALT
1 OZ (30 G) BUTTER
3 TABLESPOONS FRESHLY GRATED PARMESAN

Cook the *polenta* (p. 204), pour it into a dish and add the butter and cheese, mixing them well together. Serve.

Polenta can also be served with Gorgonzola sauce (p. 124), or it can be cooled and cut into strips, and then spread with cheese and toasted.

POLENTA FRITTA
Fried Polenta

This is a delicious way of using up cooked *polenta* – it is worth making extra so that you can have this dish for a snack later.

POLENTA (p. 204)
OLIVE OIL FOR FRYING

1. Make the *polenta* and allow it to cool in a shallow dish – it will set firmly. Cut it into 1 in (2.5 cm) squares.
2. Pour some olive oil into a large shallow frying-pan – it should be about 1 in (2.5 cm) deep – and make it very hot. Cook the *polenta* until very slightly golden and then turn it over and cook the other side. Dab it with kitchen paper when cooked.

ITALIAN SCRAMBLED EGG AND COURGETTES

Served with salad and crusty bread, this makes a good dish for lunch or supper.

To serve 4

2 MEDIUM-SIZED COURGETTES
5 EGG YOLKS AND 2 WHITES
SALT AND FRESHLY GROUND BLACK PEPPER
1 OZ (30 G) BUTTER
2 TABLESPOONS OLIVE OIL

1. Wash and dice the courgettes.
2. Put the eggs into a bowl, add the salt and pepper and beat lightly.
3. Melt the butter in a frying-pan and add the oil. When the butter is hot add the courgettes and cook for a minute. Add the beaten eggs and cook for about 3–5 minutes, moving the mixture around with a wooden spoon. Serve immediately.

FRITTATA DI ZUCCHINI
Courgette Omelette

1 OZ (30 G) UNSALTED BUTTER
1 TABLESPOON OIL
1 SMALL ONION
10 OZ (285 G) COURGETTES
SALT AND FRESHLY GROUND
  BLACK PEPPER

2 RIPE TOMATOES
2 TABLESPOONS CHICKEN
  STOCK
3 LARGE EGGS

1. Melt the butter and oil in a heavy pan and sauté the finely chopped onion.
2. Wash and slice the courgettes and add to pan with the seasoning. Remove the seeds from the tomatoes and add the chopped tomatoes to the pan; cook for 5 minutes. Add the stock and cook for a further 2 minutes.
3. Beat the eggs and add to the pan. Stir and then leave to cook until golden on one side. The eggs now should be set. Turn over and brown the other side. Serve immediately.

Fresh asparagus or potatoes can be used instead of courgettes.

UOVA AFFOGATE CON SALSA DI FUNGHI
Poached Eggs with Mushroom Sauce

This is a light lunch or supper dish that is quick and simple to prepare.

I OZ (30 G) BUTTER
I GARLIC CLOVE, CRUSHED
I TABLESPOON FRESH PARSLEY
6 OZ (170 G) SMALL WHITE
  MUSHROOMS
SALT AND FRESHLY GROUND
  BLACK PEPPER

I 14 OZ (400 G) TIN
  ITALIAN PEELED
  TOMATOES
4 LARGE EGGS, FREE-RANGE IF
  POSSIBLE
4 ROUND SLICES BREAD
4 SMALL SLICES COOKED HAM

1. Melt the butter in a shallow pan and add the garlic, parsley, sliced mushrooms and seasoning. Cook for a couple of minutes.

2. Sieve the tomatoes into the pan and boil briskly for 2 minutes. Turn down the heat and simmer for 10 minutes. Check the seasoning.

3. While the sauce is cooking poach the eggs. Put the slices of bread on a heat-proof dish, and place a slice of ham on each. When the eggs are done, put one on top of each slice of bread and ham.

4. Pour the sauce round the eggs, grind a little pepper over each and place under hot grill for about 3 minutes until the sauce is lightly browned.

PEPERONI AL FORNO
Baked Peppers

This is an unusual dish, colourful and delicious.

I YELLOW PEPPER

I GREEN PEPPER

I RED PEPPER

2 OZ (55 G) EMMENTAL CHEESE

2 MEDIUM-SIZED COURGETTES

3 OZ (85 G) COOKED HAM

½ PT (275 ML) MILK

2 EGGS

SALT AND PEPPER

NUTMEG

FRESHLY GRATED PARMESAN

1. Wash the peppers and cut them lengthwise into strips about 1½–2 in (4–5 cm) wide. Slice the Emmental very thinly and cut into squares. Cut the courgettes into thin slices.
2. Boil some water in a saucepan and cook the strips of pepper in it, a few at a time, for 2 minutes; then lift out and drain on kitchen paper.
3. Lay the peppers in a round ovenproof dish so that they hang over the sides. Cut the ham into strips and lay them directly over the peppers. Lay the squares of Emmental cheese in the centre of the dish and arrange the courgettes over the cheese.
4. Boil the milk, and then take it off the heat and add the two beaten eggs; season with salt, pepper and nutmeg.
5. Pour this over the courgettes and sprinkle with a little grated parmesan; fold the overhanging peppers and ham over the top and bake for 40 minutes at Mark 5 (375°F, 190°C).

STUFFED CABBAGE LEAVES

TOMATO SAUCE (P. 93)

8 LARGE SAVOY CABBAGE
  LEAVES

3 OZ (85 G) *RICOTTA*

2 OZ (55 G) FRESH
  BREADCRUMBS

I LEEK, CHOPPED

I EGG

SALT AND FRESHLY GROUND
  BLACK PEPPER

I TABLESPOON FRESHLY
  CHOPPED PARSLEY

3 TABLESPOONS MILK

2 TABLESPOONS GRATED
  PARMESAN

1. Prepare the tomato sauce.

2. Wash the cabbage leaves and place in boiling water for 1 minute. Drain on kitchen paper.

3. Mix all the other ingredients together in a large bowl.

4. Lay all the cabbage leaves out on a clean surface and place a heaped tablespoon of the stuffing on each. Fold the corners over, press down and tie up with string.

5. Put the stuffed cabbage leaves into a large shallow pan, pour over the sauce, bring to the boil and simmer for 20 minutes, turning occasionally.

LE VERDURE E LE INSALATE
VEGETABLE AND SALAD DISHES

In Italian homes vegetables are usually served quite plain, or sometimes dipped into batter or breadcrumbs and shallow-fried. I have given a few recipes for cooking some less familiar vegetables and also a number of recipes for salads.

PEPERONATA

This is a beautifully colourful – as well as tasty – vegetable dish, ideal for serving with any rather dull meat or fish to give it flavour.

I GREEN, I YELLOW AND I RED PEPPER
I MEDIUM–SIZED ONION
1½ OZ (45 G) BUTTER
3 TABLESPOONS OLIVE OIL
CLOVE OF GARLIC (OPTIONAL)

14 OZ (400 G) TIN ITALIAN PEELED TOMATOES, SIEVED, OR 1½ LB (0.7 KG) FRESH TOMATOES
SALT AND PEPPER

1. Discard the seeds of the peppers and cut them into ½ in (1 cm) slices. The slices do not all have to be the same size – just slice them roughly.
2. Chop the onion finely.
3. Melt the butter and oil, add the onion and garlic if used, and cook for about 2 minutes; do not let the onion burn or turn brown.
4. Add the sliced peppers and cook for a further 2 minutes. Then add the tomatoes, season and bring to a slow boil. Simmer for 30 minutes, checking for salt and stirring occasionally. Don't try to rush it, it needs at least 30 minutes' slow simmering.

AUBERGINES IN BREADCRUMBS

This is an excellent way of serving aubergines as an accompaniment for meat or fish; in fact they are good enough to serve on their own.

1 LARGE OR 2 MEDIUM-SIZED AUBERGINES
SALT
2 EGGS, WELL BEATEN
PEPPER
3–4 OZ (85–115 G) FRESH BREADCRUMBS
OLIVE OIL FOR FRYING

1. Slice the aubergines thinly. Sprinkle with salt and place in a colander with a heavy weight on top. Leave for at least 30 minutes.

2. Beat the eggs in a bowl with salt and pepper; put the breadcrumbs on a plate.

3. Pat each slice of aubergine with kitchen paper to remove the moisture.

4. Dip the slices of aubergine first into the egg mixture and then into the breadcrumbs. See that they are well covered with the breadcrumbs.

5. Heat the olive oil in a large shallow frying-pan. When it is very hot add the slices of aubergine, a few at a time, and fry until golden and crisp. Turn and fry the other side. Use kitchen paper to absorb any excess oil. Serve immediately

CARCIOFI
Artichokes

1. Wash the artichokes and cut off the stalks. Pull away any hard outer leaves and trim off the top third of each leaf.
2. Place the artichokes in boiling salted water, base downwards, and cook until done – usually about ½ hour; they are ready when the heart is soft. (The cooking time obviously depends on the size and age of the artichoke.)

If they are to be served cold, place them in cold water immediately.

In Italy artichokes are often eaten cold, sprinkled with a little olive oil and seasoned with salt and pepper. The leaves are peeled off one by one, and the hard part discarded.

To prepare artichoke hearts

Pull off the outside leaves and trim as evenly as possible, so that only the middle fleshy part remains. Really young artichokes should be easily stripped down to their hearts. Remove the choke and trim the hearts; rub each well with a cut lemon and place in cold water as soon as you have trimmed it.

Cooked artichoke hearts can be served in salad with a dressing or may be served hot with a sauce.

TOPINAMBUR
Jerusalem Artichokes

Jerusalem artichokes look rather like ginger root. They should be firm and whitish under the skin. They must be peeled, and this does take some time if you have a lot to peel and they are particularly curly ones. They can be eaten raw, usually finely grated, in salads. There is a recipe for artichoke sauce to eat with pasta on p. 100.

PATATE CON ROSMARINO
Potatoes with Rosemary

This may sound an extravagant way of cooking potatoes in olive oil but it is worth it – once you have tried potatoes cooked in this way you will never be able to resist them.

To serve 4–6

2 LB (0.9 KG) POTATOES (SUITABLE FOR FRYING)
$\frac{3}{4}$ PINT OLIVE OIL
A FEW SPRIGS OF FRESH ROSEMARY
SALT

1. Peel and wash the potatoes and pat them dry with kitchen paper.
2. Cut them into pieces – they do not have to be uniform, or even a regular shape.
3. In a large shallow frying pan heat the oil until it is very hot. Add the rosemary – if the oil is hot enough to cook the potatoes it will sizzle. Add the potatoes carefully and cook on a high heat for about 7–8 minutes. Obviously the time will vary with the type of potatoes used and their size. When cooked the potatoes should be a light golden brown colour and cooked all the way through.
4. Lift the potatoes out on to kitchen paper with a slotted spoon. Dab off the oil, sprinkle very lightly with salt and serve immediately.

Do not leave the potatoes in the oven to keep warm as they will lose their crispness. They can be served with almost any meat or fish dish but are especially good with plain grilled trout and a crisp green salad.

SALADS

Use your best olive oil for salads, as the flavour of the oil is important to the dish. If you have any fresh herbs to hand they will enhance any salad.

Make your salad in a generous-sized bowl so that you have plenty of room for turning it.

INSALATA VERDE
Plain Green Salad

1 CRISP LETTUCE
OLIVE OIL
WINE VINEGAR
SALT

The amount of olive oil, vinegar and salt used is really a matter of taste. To make the salad, wash the lettuce and dry thoroughly and then either tear the leaves or chop or shred them. Put the lettuce into a bowl and add the olive oil and then the vinegar and salt. If you are not used to adding the vinegar direct, add a very small amount only and then mix the salad and taste.

Put the salad in a cool place – not the refrigerator – and let it stand for at least $\frac{1}{2}$ hour before eating.

INSALATA DI RADICCHIO
Radicchio Salad

I RADICCHIO LETTUCE

OLIVE OIL

WINE VINEGAR

SALT AND FRESHLY GROUND BLACK PEPPER

Wash and dry the radicchio and either tear it into small pieces or slice it. Put it into a serving-dish and add enough olive oil to coat. Add a little wine vinegar to taste and season with the salt and pepper; mix together well.

Do not refrigerate. Prepare at least ½ hour before serving. You can also add green lettuce to give more colour to the dish.

INSALATA DI POMIDORI
Tomato Salad

If possible, try to buy the large beef or slicing tomatoes to make this salad – they really do have a much better flavour, and after they have soaked in olive oil for a while they are truly delicious. Alternatively, you can use small, sweet cherry tomatoes.

2 LARGE BEEF TOMATOES
ENOUGH OLIVE OIL TO COAT THE TOMATOES
SALT AND FRESHLY GROUND BLACK PEPPER
A FEW LEAVES OF FRESH BASIL
A FEW DROPS OF WINE VINEGAR, TO TASTE

Wash and dry the tomatoes, and cut them into slices, removing the green bit. Put them into a dish, add the olive oil, vinegar and seasoning and the fresh basil leaves torn in half. Leave for at least 1 hour before serving. Do not refrigerate.

FAGIOLINI CON TONNO
Beans and Tuna

This combination of French beans and tuna makes a fairly substantial *antipasto*; it also goes well with cold meat as a salad.

1 LB (450 G) FRENCH BEANS
OLIVE OIL
LEMON JUICE
6 OZ (170 G) TIN TUNA
SALT AND FRESHLY GROUND BLACK PEPPER

1. Prepare and cook the beans but do not let them get soft — for this recipe it is important that the beans are not overcooked.
2. Leave the beans to cool for a few minutes and while they are still warm pour some olive oil over them (just enough to coat the beans) and add a little lemon juice.
3. Add the tuna in small pieces, season and mix well.

INSALATA DI FAGIOLI
Mixed Bean Salad

½ LB (225 G) FRESH GREEN
  BEANS
3 OZ (85 G) DRIED KIDNEY
  BEANS
3 OZ (85 G) DRIED BUTTER OR
  LIMA BEANS
OLIVE OIL

RED WINE VINEGAR
SALT AND FRESHLY GROUND
  PEPPER
I TABLESPOON CHOPPED FRESH
  PARSLEY

1. Soak overnight and boil the dried beans for 20 minutes.
2. Wash the green beans and top and tail them. Put into boiling water and cook for about 5–8 minutes – they should be cooked, but still crisp. Drain well and put to one side.
3. Put all the beans, dried and fresh, into a large serving-dish and add the olive oil, vinegar, seasoning and parsley. Serve with cold meat.

INSALATA DI FAGIOLINI
Green Bean Salad

1 LB (450 G) GREEN BEANS
OLIVE OIL
SALT AND FRESHLY GROUND BLACK PEPPER
FRESH LEMON JUICE (OPTIONAL)

1. Wash the beans and top and tail them. Bring some water to the boil, add the beans and boil for 8–10 minutes.
2. Drain and allow to cool for 10 minutes. Put the beans in a bowl and add some olive oil and salt and pepper. You can also add fresh lemon juice, if desired

Serve while still warm.

INSALATA DI FUNGHI CON ACCIUGHE
Mushroom and Anchovy Salad

1 LB (450 G) FRESH MUSHROOMS
OLIVE OIL
LEMON JUICE
FRESHLY GROUND BLACK PEPPER
ABOUT 6 ANCHOVY FILLETS

1. Wash the mushrooms, drain and slice thinly.
2. Put them into a serving-dish, adding enough olive oil to coat them. Sprinkle with a little lemon juice and add some black pepper; mix well.
3. Just before serving chop the anchovy fillets and add to the mushrooms.

INSALATA DI PATATE
Potato Salad

6 MEDIUM-SIZED POTATOES
6–8 TABLESPOONS OLIVE OIL
SALT AND FRESHLY GROUND BLACK PEPPER
1 TABLESPOON LEMON JUICE

Clean the potatoes and boil them in their skins until they are cooked but still firm.

Peel them immediately and dice them while still warm. Add the olive oil, salt, pepper and lemon juice.

This is a basic recipe for potato salad – fresh herbs, especially mint, capers or very thinly sliced onions, for instance, can be added.

INSALATA DI PEPERONI
Pepper Salad

I GREEN PEPPER

I YELLOW PEPPER

I RED PEPPER

OLIVE OIL

I CLOVE OF GARLIC

SALT AND FRESHLY GROUND

  BLACK PEPPER

I TABLESPOON CHOPPED

  PARSLEY

1. Bake the peppers at Mark 5 (375°F, 190°C) for about 30 minutes. Peel the peppers and cut them into strips; discard any seeds and pith.

2. Place the peppers in a serving-dish, adding the olive oil, crushed garlic, seasoning and parsley.

Leave for 30 minutes – do not refrigerate.

INSALATA DI RADICCHIO E CANNELLINI
Salad of Radicchio and Cannellini Beans

For this recipe you can use either dry cannellini beans soaked overnight and boiled for 45 minutes or tinned cannellini.

I RADICCHIO LETTUCE

I TIN CANNELLINI BEANS OR 4 OZ (115 G) DRIED BEANS

OLIVE OIL

WINE VINEGAR

SALT AND FRESHLY GROUND BLACK PEPPER

1. If using dried beans, soak them overnight and boil them for 20 minutes. Drain and alow to cool.
2. Wash and dry the radicchio. Tear the leaves into pieces, put them into a bowl and add the beans.
3. Add the olive oil and the wine vinegar and seasoning, and mix together. Leave for 30 minutes in a cool place but not the fridge.

INSALATA DI ZUCCHINI E FAGIOLINI
Courgette and Bean Salad

1 LB (450 G) GREEN BEANS
2 MEDIUM-SIZED COURGETTES
OLIVE OIL
SALT AND PEPPER

1. Top and tail the beans; wash the courgettes and slice them diagonally.
2. Bring a pan of water to the boil, add the beans and cook for 1 minute. Then add the courgettes and cook for another minute. Drain and leave to cool for 10 minutes.
3. Put the beans and courgettes into a bowl and add olive oil to taste and the seasoning. Mix well and serve.

This salad is best when the courgettes and beans are still slightly warm.

I Dolci
Sweets

Fruit grows in abundance in Italy, and in Italian homes a meal almost invariably ends with fresh fruit and cheese; more elaborate desserts are kept for special occasions.

In restaurants, sweets often consist of fruit tarts, cakes or ices – the Italians are, of course, famous for the excellence of their ice-cream. The bakers' shops are filled with cakes, tarts and biscuits in amazing variety. Each region has its own specialities.

Tins of *amaretti*, almond-flavoured macaroons, are sometimes available in delicatessens in England, and also *panettone*, traditionally eaten at Christmas in Italy, packed in festive boxes. (*Panettone* is a very light yeast cake with sultanas and crystallized peel in it; it is usually accompanied by Asti Spumante.) At Christmas time you may also be able to find *panforte di Siena*, a rich, dense cake full of candied fruit and nuts, and flavoured with spices and orange peel. *Columba*, the traditional Easter cake, is a plain, light yeast cake, sweeter than *panettone*. It is often made in the shape of a dove and, like *panettone*, it is attractively packed.

MACEDONIA DI FRUTTA
Fruit Salad

Italians eat lots of fruit salad, using whatever fruit is in season; the recipe can be varied according to what is available. If you are using well-coloured red apples you can leave the peel on so that they add colour to the fruit salad.

It is a good idea to make fruit salad the night before you want to eat it, or in the morning, so that the flavour has time to develop.

3 APPLES	3 ORANGES, SQUEEZED
2 PEARS	2 BANANAS
2 PEACHES (MUST BE RIPE)	1–2 OZ (30–55 G) SUGAR, OR
A BUNCH OF GRAPES	TO TASTE
2 LEMONS, SQUEEZED	

1. Wash the apples and peel them if you want to; peel the pears. Cut the apples and pears into quarters and remove the cores. Peel the peaches, cut in half and remove the stones. Remove the seeds of the grapes.
2. Squeeze the oranges and lemons and pour the juice into a large serving-bowl.
3. Cut the apples, pears, peaches and bananas into smallish cubes and add to the dish with the grapes. Add the sugar and mix well. Refrigerate or place in a cool larder for 3 hours or longer, but remove from the fridge at least 1 hour before serving.

FRAGOLE AL VINO ROSSO
Strawberries in Red Wine

Don't be tempted to use plonk for this dish — it is worth using a reasonably good wine.

To serve 4

I LB (450 G) STRAWBERRIES
4 GLASSES FULL-BODIED RED WINE
SUGAR

You can either put all the ingredients in a serving-dish or, more informally, just serve the strawberries with a bowl of sugar and four glasses of red wine, and let everyone drop strawberries into their wine with as much sugar as they like.

PESCHE IN VINO BIANCO
Peaches in White Wine

Let everyone have a glass of white wine – it should not be too dry, Pinot Grigio would be ideal – and a ripe peach. Peel and slice the peaches and drop the slices into the wine. What could be simpler!

PESCHE RIPIENE
Stuffed Peaches

To serve 4

4 MEDIUM–SIZED PEACHES
2 TABLESPOONS CHOPPED ALMONDS
2 TABLESPOONS RAISINS
½ TEASPOON CINNAMON
I TABLESPOON SOFT BROWN SUGAR
I TABLESPOON LEMON JUICE

1. Cut each peach in half and remove the stones and some of the pulp to make room for the stuffing. Retain the pulp.
2. Mix all the other ingredients including the pulp together in a bowl.
3. Stuff each peach with the mixture, place on a buttered tray and bake for 25 minutes at Mark 5 (375°F, 190°C).

PESCHE RIPIENE CON AMARETTI
Peaches Stuffed with Macaroons

To serve 4

4 MEDIUM-SIZED PEACHES
I TABLESPOON ALMONDS, CRUSHED
3 OZ (85 G) MACAROONS, CRUSHED — USE ITALIAN *AMARETTI*
　IF YOU CAN GET THEM
I TABLESPOON BROWN SUGAR
I OZ (30 G) MELTED BUTTER
I SMALL EGG YOLK

1. Cut the peaches in half and remove the stones and some of the pulp to make room for the filling. Retain the pulp.
2. Mix all the other ingredients with the pulp in a bowl.
3. Stuff each peach with the mixture, place on a buttered tray and bake for 25 minutes at Mark 5 (375°F, 190°C).

CREMA DI MASCARPONE

Use this instead of cream to accompany fresh soft fruit such as strawberries and raspberries.

To serve 4–6

6 OZ (170 G) ITALIAN *MASCARPONE*
2 EGG YOLKS
2 OZ (55 G) SUGAR
2 TABLESPOONS *AMARETTO*

Put the *mascarpone* and egg yolks into a bowl and whisk well together. You can use an electric hand whisk for this. Add the sugar and *amaretto* and mix again.

NB. If you do not have *amaretto* you can use another spirit instead, such as kirsch or cognac. Or add some very finely chopped fresh mint.

BANANE FIAMMANTI
Flambé Bananas

A LITTLE BUTTER

4 BANANAS

2 ORANGES

1 OZ (30 G) SUGAR

4 TABLESPOONS RUM

1. Line a lightly buttered dish with the bananas, pour over the juice of the oranges and sprinkle with sugar. Leave in the fridge for 1 hour.
2. Pour over the rum. Ignite and serve immediately.

TORTA DI MELE
Apple Pudding

2 EGGS	MILK
6 OZ (170 G) SUGAR	12 G FRESH YEAST
7½ OZ (215 G) FLOUR	BREADCRUMBS
RIND OF 1 LEMON, GRATED	2 LB APPLES

1. Beat the eggs and sugar together well. Add the flour sifted with the lemon rind, and 2 tablespoons of milk.
2. Mix in the yeast.
3. Lightly butter a baking tray and sprinkle it with breadcrumbs. Pour in the egg and flour mixture.
4. Peel and slice the apples and arrange on top. Sprinkle with a little sugar and a few dabs of butter. Bake at Mark 5 (375°F, 190°C) for 30 minutes.

Eat hot or cold.

ZABAGLIONE

This is one of the classics of Italian cookery. Because it is made with eggs it must not be allowed to boil or the eggs will curdle, so for your first attempt it is a good idea to cook the *zabaglione* in a double boiler or a heavy pan over boiling water. In Italy *zabaglione* is often cooked in copper pans shaped like funnels.

To serve 6

4 LARGE EGG YOLKS
1½ OZ (45 G) CASTER SUGAR
6 TABLESPOONS MARSALA

1. Beat the egg yolks and sugar together in a heavy pan until pale yellow and frothy.
2. Place the pan with the egg mixture in it over a pan of boiling water, add the marsala and beat continuously until the mixture has thickened slightly and is foamy. Pour into fluted glasses and serve immediately.

Tiramisù
Mascarpone *and Chocolate Pudding*

Tiramisù means 'pick-me-up'. It is quite delicious and very simple to make. There are many variations on the recipe, but the basic ingredients are always the same.

¼ PT (150 ML) FRESHLY
GROUND STRONG BLACK
ITALIAN COFFEE
250 G TUB *MASCARPONE*
2 TABLESPOONS BROWN SUGAR

3 EGGS
5 OZ (115 G) GRATED
CHOCOLATE
200 G PACK SAVOIARDI
ITALIAN SPONGE FINGERS

1. Make the coffee, empty it into a bowl and allow it to cool completely.
2. In a food processor or a large bowl, mix the *mascarpone*, sugar and eggs thoroughly. Add the grated chocolate, leaving two tablespoons for decoration.
3. Dip the biscuits very quickly into the cold coffee and lay them flat in a shallow serving-dish. Do not submerge the biscuits as they will become too soggy.
4. Pour some of the *mascarpone* mixture over the biscuits. Continue with another layer of biscuits and another layer of *mascarpone*, and so on until all the biscuits are used. Finish with a thick layer of the *mascarpone* mixture. Sprinkle with the grated chocolate and refrigerate for at least 3 hours. Remove from the refrigerator ½ hour before serving.

CHOCOLATE MINT MOUSSE

3½ OZ (100 G) DARK COOKING CHOCOLATE
1 OZ (30 G) BUTTER
3 EGGS, SEPARATED
1 TEASPOON CHOPPED FRESH MINT, AND EXTRA MINT FOR
   DECORATION

1. Break up the chocolate, put it into a dish over a pan of boiling water, add the butter and leave until melted.
2. Separate the eggs and beat the yolk.
3. Chop the mint finely. Whisk the egg-whites until stiff.
4. When the chocolate is completely melted, remove it from heat and beat in the egg yolks and 1 tablespoon warm water.
5. Stir in a tablespoon of the whisked egg white. (This makes it easier to combine the chocolate and egg white.) Carefully fold in the rest of the egg white with a metal spoon.
6. Add 1 teaspoon of the chopped mint and pour into individual dishes. Refrigerate for at least 4 hours. Decorate with mint before serving.

BUDINO AL LIMONE
Lemon Mousse

1 LEMON
3 OZ (85 G) SUGAR
1 OZ (30 G) BUTTER
4 EGGS

1. Boil the whole lemon for $\frac{1}{2}$ hour in about a teacup of water. Squeeze out the lemon into the water, removing the pips.
2. Add the sugar, butter and egg yolks and beat. Whisk the egg whites and fold in gently.
3. Pour the mixture into a mould and bake at Mark 5 (375°F, 190°C) in a roasting tin with water in it for approximately 20 minutes.

Serve cold.

BUDINO DI RICOTTA

8 OZ (225 G) FRESH
  RICOTTA CHEESE
2 OZ (55 G) SUGAR
2 OZ (55 G) CRUSHED
  ALMONDS
A FEW *AMARETTI* BISCUITS,
  CRUSHED

4 EGG WHITES, WHISKED
2 TABLESPOONS LEMON JUICE
1 OZ (30 G) BREADCRUMBS

1. Either liquidize the *ricotta* or put it through a sieve.
2. Mix the sugar, almonds, *amaretti* and whisked egg white with the *ricotta* and lemon juice.
3. Butter a cake tin or ovenproof dish well and pour in the mixture, sprinkle with the breadcrumbs and cook at Mark 5 (375°F, 190°C) for 30 minutes.

Serve cold.

INDEX